Fe̶̶̶̶̶

# THE GREATER APHRODISIAD

The author left Oxford without a degree to serve in the Royal Navy during the Second World War. Afterwards he was employed successively by the Foreign Office and the Ministry of Defence. His other writings include *Corsican Excursion* (Bodley Head, 1952), *History of West Dean Church and Parish* (6th Edition 1977), *St Paul's Wood Green, The First Hundred Years* (1973), (Editor) *A Lady of Wednesbury Forge* (Black Country Society, 1976) and *Aspects of the Black Country* (Black Country Society, 1991). *Tracts Beyond the Times* (Social Affairs Unit, 1983) is among the author's writings on aspects of contemporary politics.

# THE GREATER APHRODISIAD

## or

# MAJORCA

*I have found out a rich people before not known, and discovered a great kingdom till then concealed.*

Emperor Charles the Fifth

## Charles J.L. Elwell

With Illustrations by
## J.B. Laurens and Gustave Doré

FERRINGTON, BOOKSELLER & PUBLISHER
LONDON
1995

First published 1995
Copyright © Charles Elwell 1995
All rights reserved.


ISBN 1-898490-16-3


Ferrington, Bookseller & Publisher
The Bookshop, 31-35 Gt Ormond St.
London WC1N 3HZ


*Typeset by Saxon Graphics Ltd, Derby*
*Printed and bound in Great Britain*
*by Biddles Ltd, Guildford and King's Lynn.*

# CONTENTS

## ILLUSTRATIONS

# ACKNOWLEDGEMENTS

My thanks are due for information and for other assistance that has been most kindly given to me by Mrs F.W. Latrobe Bateman; Mr John Latrobe Bateman; Señor D. Miguel Bota Totxo; Señor D. Alejandro Cuellar Bassols, Secretary of the Ayuntamiento of La Puebla; Messrs William Heinemann, who allowed me to quote from The Letters of D.H. Lawrence; Señor D. Juan Muntaner, Cronista Official de Palma y Reino de Mallorca; Señor D. Juan Pons y Marques, Director del Archivo Histórico de Mallorca and Señor D. Portman, Manager of the Hotel Formentor. I am particularly grateful to the late Robert Graves for his generous help and encouragement, to the Marquesa de Valdueza for lending me her splendidly bound copy of her grandfather's book, *Viaje a Mallorca*, to Mrs Jennifer Botsford for information about her mother and the Centro Canino Internacional, and to my publisher for his many suggestions for the improvement of the text.

# PROLOGUE

When the illustrious lovers, Chopin and George Sand, went to Majorca a century and a half ago, they probably did not realise that their choice of a romantic retreat had been so appropriate. They may have heard that the Island's warriors were formidable slingers (Ballesteros) in Roman times, like the inhabitants of that other 'Balearic' island of Portland, but they were almost certainly unaware of the Majorcan's legendary preoccupation with love. It was only later that George Sand discovered that, if Majorca was the Greater of the Balearics, it was also the Greater of the Aphrodisiads. This name was used by the two learned Saints, Jerome and Isidore of Seville, "because Venus called by the Greeks Aphrodite was adored there".

The Saints' information was derived largely from the writings of Greek and Roman geographers, and it is to the former that the inhabitants of the Balearics owe their reputation for being excessively fond of women, a reputation that still persists. According to the Greeks, the islanders went naked during the summer months and for this reason they called the islands "the Gymnesiæ". This nudism, due to the summer heat, may have been partly responsible, contrary to what we are led to believe by modern advocates of the practice, for certain remarkable customs described by Strabo and others. Basing himself on their authority, Dameto, Majorca's first native historian, states that the islanders were "so much inclined to women that for one of that sex they will give in exchange three or four men... When they went to war with the Carthagians [sic] (with whom they were in alliance), they used to exchange their wages and pay for wine and women. But what is more to be wondered at is a custom they observe in their marriages; for their kinsmen and friends, according to their age, enjoy the bride first and afterwards pass the time in drinking healths to the patient husband."*

A reputation once acquired is difficult to live down and modern Majorcans have not quite succeeded in shedding the reputation which was first given to their forefathers by the Greeks and Romans, kept alive by Saints Jerome and Isidore, and handed down by their own first historian to almost every foreigner who has since written about them. The Rev. Henry Christmas, to take only one example, writing of Majorcan morals in 1851, is obliged regretfully to note that "there is a good deal of indifference among them as to personal virtue which is the greatest if not the sole failing with which they are generally chargeable."

It would not be possible to prove that what the Greeks said about the primitive inhabitants of the island, is true of contemporary Majorcans, who would be the first to deny the charge with horror. To some observers they have even succeeded in giving the impression that the island, so far from being dedicated to Venus, is firmly tied to the apron strings of Mrs Grundy. The notices displayed in public buildings, enjoining on visitors a certain minimum standard of decency in their dress, might perhaps account for such an impression. It is not however from mere prudery that the Majorcan endeavours to prevent the uninhibited tourist from unconsciously imitating the summer habits of the ancient inhabitants of the Gymnesiæ as soon as he or she feels the blessed warmth of the Mediterranean sun. His motives are more aesthetic than moral.

---

*The Ancient and Modern History of the Balearic Islands Based on the Works of Juan Dameto and Vicente Mut. Translated by Colin Campbell with the Help of Mr Hammond. London 1716.

Regarding, as he does, the avenues and promenades of his cities and towns as parade grounds for the display and enjoyment of such elegance as is available, he prefers that the passing show should not be spoilt by the intrusion of uncouth and blatant nudity. But the clearest indication that "decency" rules are not a manifestation of a Puritan outlook, is to be found on the beaches where the briefest of Bikinis are permitted to expose the maximum of flesh, and where fugitives from white-collared Northern mists may offer themselves wantonly as burnt sacrifices to the sun.

Those who are determined to convict Majorcans of their reputed failing have seen evidence of it in the excessively amorous record of some of their kings and the historian Dameto is called again to bear witness. Writing of Jaime the Conquistador, the founder of Christian Majorca, he says, "To some it would appear that he sullied his bright qualities a little in his youth, by giving way to disorderly amours in which he was often entangled. He that was invulnerable to the fiercest darts of Mars became a slave to the arrows of Cupid!" "But this," concludes the historian comfortably, "is a fault so much the easier to be excused, it being a folly but too alluring and agreeable to our weak and deprav'd natures." King Sancho too seems to have been a merry fellow, but if we tried to measure the lasciviousness of the Majorcans by the immorality of some of their monarchs, they would compare very favourably with, for example, the subjects of Louis XIV and Louis XV and their descendants.

The career of Majorca's national hero and saint, Raymond Lull, would furnish the detractors of Majorcan morals with a better illustration of their case. Though the story of this great man's conversion from rake to saint is well-known and is repeated in almost every book on Majorca, I should not feel justified if I were to omit it from this one. It seems appropriate too, in view of the context, to make use of the version recorded by that master of the amorous anecdote Pierre de Brantôme.

"We have a fine example of this (beautiful women sometimes not being so beautiful when uncovered) in the story of a nobleman of Majorca, called Raymond Lull, of very good, rich and ancient lineage who, because of his nobility, valour and virtue, was summoned in his prime to be governor of the island. While occupying this position, as often happens to governors of provinces and cities, he fell in love with a beautiful lady, one of the cleverest, fairest and most gracious in the island. He paid court to her for a long time and right well; and was always begging to her for the ultimate enjoyment. She, after having refused him as well as she might, one day gave him a rendezvous, which they both kept, and where she seemed more beautiful and desirable than ever. Just as he thought he was about to enter paradise, she laid bare her breast, which was covered with a dozen plasters, and, tearing them off one after the other and throwing them on to the ground, she displayed to him a frightful cancer and with tears in her eyes, bewailed her misery and sickness, asking him if there was now really good reason for him to love her so passionately; and then she spoke to him so sorrowfully that he, being overcome with pity for this beautiful lady in her distress, left her; and having recommended her to God for her health, gave up his position and became a hermit."

It is however a far cry from the days of Jaime the Conquistador and Raymond Lull and it would be unreasonable to judge contemporary Majorcans by the youthful follies of some of their ancestors. Nevertheless, one cannot help feeling that the Majorcan Tourist Office's poster recommending one to "Honeymoon in Majorca" argues a perhaps subconscious admission that Aphrodite is indeed the pagan patron of the island and that the sunshine, the blue sea, the aromatic hill-sides, the well-cultivated valleys, the corn and wine and oil and plenty all conspire to do her service.

> *Aqui hay luz, vida. Hay un mar*
> *De cobalto aqui, y un sol*
> *Que estimula entre las venas*
> *Sangre de pagano amor.*

> Here there is light, life. Here a sea
> Of cobalt, and a sun
> Which stimulates within the veins
> The blood of pagan love.

This was how Rubén Darío felt about Majorca, but it is not necessary to be a Nicaraguan and a great Spanish poet to feel something of this stimulation and even if you do not travel to Majorca under Aphrodite's auspices you will scarcely fail to be at least partially initiated to her rites by falling in love with the island itself.

# CHAPTER I
## THE VILLA

*"Formentor, the most beautiful spot in the world."*
Hotel Advertisement

The morning of our arrival at the Villa was cold and grey and we had expected that April 1st in Majorca would be warm and sunny. Had she by any chance made fools of us? The sea looked not blue, but dull and uninviting and much too far away from the Villa, down the pine clad slope of Formentor Bay. There was no hot water in the taps and there were no cots for the two smallest children. There was food but no strong drink. We felt very depressed. Had we perhaps been too rash in taking the Villa merely on the strength of an advertisement in the Agony Column of The Times and two short letters in halting English from our prospective landlord? What should we do with the children if there were no cots for them to sleep in? Would our expected guests enjoy staying in a house where there was no hot water? What was the point anyway in coming to Majorca if the weather made it seem just like England? The whole point surely of coming to this Mediterranean pearl was that we did not particularly want to be in England now that April was there. This was our introduction to Majorca; full of doubts and forebodings. We could not have supposed on that first morning, when we were weary after an uneasy night's crossing from Barcelona to Palma, that the Villa which then appeared so cold, solitary and uninviting, could have become a place of warmth, repose and cheerful enchantment.

The Villa stands among Corsican pines about a hundred and fifty yards up the steep slope that enfolds the western end of Formentor Bay. Rectangular in shape and built on two floors, it dates from the 1930's and in its style of architecture has vague affinities with Lutyens. Its walls are of the local sandstone coated with rough cast, which has been bleached white by the sun. At one end there is a tiled balcony as large as a room - a perfect retreat for sunbathers. The windows are flanked with jalousies painted, appropriately I have just realised, a deep green. They were shut during the heat of the day to keep the rooms moderately cool. On three sides of the Villa there is a terrace of rust red tiles with a cement balustrade, where we would sit and sun ourselves and drink and admire the view of and from "the most beautiful spot in the world". Below us were the waters of Formentor Bay, which forms a small indentation in the greater bay or rather gulf of Pollensa beyond. The sea was often blue, the colour of turquoise or sapphire or aquamarine, but sometimes it was green like verdigris. Often the surface would be disturbed by eddies and currents and the ripples they caused would now and then form shapes and outlines of sea serpents and other marine monsters perhaps on holiday from Loch Ness. The far side of Pollensa Bay is bounded by the hills of the spit of land known as Punta de la Victoria, that divides Pollensa from Alcudia Bay. Where it joins the mainland the hills cease and on this flat piece of country is situated the ancient city of Alcudia. On clear days its great church stood like another small hill sharply outlined against the blue sky.

Formentor Bay is dominated by two mountains or hills that deserve to be called mountains: to the west the Falda de na Blanca, a great sugar loaf some 950ft high on whose lower slopes the Villa lay and to the east the loftier but much less impressive hill of Albercuitz, crowned by its canister-shaped watch

1

tower. Both of these mountains put us on our mettle and were to be the scenes of strenuous ascents by various members of the party.

The air we breathed, as we sat on the terrace basking in the sun and gazing seawards over sips of Spanish gin, was heavy with aromatic scents, pine, lentiscus, rosemary and myrtle. Among the trees and shrubs birds twittered and chirruped, and their song was often the only sound that disturbed the forest silence around the Villa. Sometimes in the early morning we would be aroused by the tinkling of sheep bells as a flock passed beneath our windows and at night we would be kept awake by the loud and sustained warbles of the nightingale, which were frequently rivalled and in some respects surpassed by the even louder warbles of one of the children, awakened by unheeding Philomel.

These sounds were the regular accompaniment of our lives at the Villa and there were others also of a slightly less pastoral timbre. There were sporadic gobble-gobbles from a turkey who lived at a villa in another part of the forest, there were the choppings of woodsmen's axes when they worked nearby and there was with regrettably increasing frequency the sound of motor cars and motor coaches passing, invisible to us, along the dusty road below, bearing loads of tourists to the Hotel for a brief visit to the sands of the Bay.

These incursions from the outside world were nevertheless still so rare and remote that they hardly diluted the isolation in which we lived. We had no telephone and no wireless, there were no newspapers and no post and the nearest shop was five miles away on the other side of a steep mountain pass. Our food came every morning in a boat from Puerto Pollensa and this was the only way we could get it unless we drove to the Puerto in the car - for there was no public transport at all, and the only motor vehicle that was ever to be seen using the rough road that went past the Villa was the lorry from the sawmill at Pollensa.

This isolation of ours was however a comfortable isolation, comparable, if the imagination were worked a little, to that which was enjoyed several centuries ago in Italy by Boccacio's "seven ladies and gentlemen" who made themselves "innocently merry" for ten days in a place of retirement. A large part of their enjoyment was surely due to their having been able to bring their servants with them. Their story-telling, one feels, would scarcely have been such a success had it not been for the expert ministrations of Parmeno, Chimera and their colleagues. They would certainly not have "dined with all the facetiousness imaginable" if they had known they had to wash up after it. Nor were they the sort of people who would have enjoyed a caravan holiday or a camping holiday or least of all, a really good hiking holiday. They would not have relished messes out of a battered billy-can or steaming brews from chipped enamel mugs. Such healthful rigours would not have suited them, and a certain leisured elegance combined with a freedom from the brute necessities of life were essential to their delightful story-telling.

To some extent we found or achieved this at the Villa. Elegance, if only superficial or an illusion of it, was created by the interior of the house, with its magnificent crystal chandeliers, one of which was suspended in the *salon* perilously like the sword of Damocles by a piece of wire to a small hook that peeped precariously from the ceiling. To look at it made one feel like a man hanging on by his finger tips and one instinctively avoided sitting directly under it. The furniture tended to disprove George Sand's assertion that the Majorcans had lost the art of cabinet making. The tables and chairs of unpolished oak were admirably designed and beautifully made, while the beds with their high carved backs like the reredos of some pagan altar would have formed a worthy setting equally for the merriment of a marriage night in the Greater Aphrodisiad or the flickering gloom of the viaticum in the mustiest bedchamber of Castile.

Comfort in some respects was not exactly thrust upon us, nor did we always achieve it. Water was a constant problem as indeed it is and always has been in most parts of Majorca. There is either too much of it, or not enough, but generally the latter. The Moors did a great deal to tap, conserve and distribute such supplies of water as are available and their methods and even their appliances in many cases are still used today.*

The Villa's water system, though more modern than these, was in some respects less reliable. It was connected to the pipe which carried water to the Hotel, but before water could flow from a tap, it had to be pumped up to a cistern on the roof. This cistern not being very big and the demand for water being insatiable, the pump which was electric had to be set to work at frequent intervals. After dinner was a favourite time for it to be turned on and we never failed to be startled when the evening calm was shattered by the roar of the pump as it shuddered protestingly into life. From time to time it would break down and our water supply would be cut off. Then urgent messages would be sent down to the Hotel and in due course Pedro el Albeñil (the bricklayer) or his colleague, the Hotel plumber, would ascend to the Villa and fix up the pump so that it worked once more for a week or two.

The Villa's water system was the principal source of what little discomfort we suffered and, because of its vagaries, hot baths were a comparative rarity, though in such a climate and in such a place, the lack of them was not a severe deprivation. Trifling plumbing mishaps such as blocked pipes also occurred periodically but a more serious source of irritation was the great number of flies that appeared when the weather got warmer. At one moment we were quite concerned at the rate at which they were multiplying but a Spanish insecticide of notable virulence, which we had ordered urgently from the Puerto, was soon effective in keeping their numbers down.

The discomforts we endured were however insignificant in comparison with the comforts we enjoyed, and the chief promoter of these was Francisca, the cook, assisted by Madalena, the housemaid and later by her successor Marcelina. The general consensus of opinion among foreigners who have written about their experiences in Majorca, seems to be that Majorcan servants are bad. They have been accused of being dirty, idle, grasping and prone to petty thieving. George Sand complained that she was obliged to keep her precious groceries, which she had obtained with considerable difficulty from Palma, under lock and key in order to preserve them from the light fingers of her domestics. Thomas Bidwell, the British Consul at Palma in the 1860's, who had four years' experience of the island, devotes several pages of his book and some feeling to the awfulness of Majorcan servants, whom he compared unfavourably with their English counterparts. He says "it would be a flattering comparison as regards domestic servants in these islands to say that the combined services of two native men, or those of three women were equal to those of one English man or maid servant." He was writing in 1864 when English servants may have been better, as they were more plentiful,

*True in 1954.

than they are now, but even in 1911 Mrs Boyd felt obliged to state "that it would be futile to expect to find the carefully drilled attendance with which home usage has accustomed us" and "to our more conservative mind, the attitude of the island servitors towards their employers seems strangely familiar." As late as 1927 the waspish Frederick Chamberlin, complaining generally about Majorcan servants, inveighed against their extreme dirtiness. Yet in the same year his American compatriot Nina Larrey Duryea assured her readers that "Servants are easily obtained and are amiable, clean and ignorant", while some twenty years later Lady Sheppard not only stressed the passion for cleanliness of the Majorcan housewife but described at length the overall excellence of her domestic staff.

Our experience happily coincided with Lady Sheppard's and though Francisca herself must of course be unique, we had it on her supreme authority that there were other cooks, who were as good as she. Francisca was a stout strongly built woman with greying hair, a high complexion and the kindest eyes that smiled at you - they could also glare wrathfully - through a pair of black rimmed spectacles. She was a most lovable person, who seemed to fill the house with the warmth of her nature as she filled it so frequently with the delicious aromas from her cooking. The children loved her and she would play with them and talk to them in Spanish - which no doubt she thought they would understand more easily than Majorcan - and pick them up, hugging them to her majestic bosom, wishing they were hers, for her only baby had died.

A good deal has been written about the excessive familiarity of Majorcan servants with their employers, but no one would have accused Francisca, Madalena, or Marcelina of such a failing. Francisca's manner of addressing us was so extremely formal that at first it led to some slight confusion. Not only did she not presume, when talking to me, to use the sufficiently polite Spanish "usted", deeming it more correct to address me as "El Señor", but she also referred to herself as "La Servidora". Thus, though it may have been clear enough who "El Señor" was, we were by no means certain, at least in the early stages of our acquaintance, who "La Servidora" was. At first we supposed Francisca was talking about the housemaid or perhaps even about a servant in some other house, until the context made it clear that it was herself to whom she was referring.

The impeccable manners of the Majorcans were approved by the great Spanish writer Miguel de Unamuno, who thought them much better than those of the Castilians. He says that when he was in Majorca, now over seventy years ago, it was customary for the driver of a country cart to make way for a motor car wishing to pass, by driving into the side of the road, standing up and bowing as he did so. In Castile, on the other hand, the impatient motorist was more likely to be reviled with curses by the muleteer, whom he was so rash as to try and overtake. Should the Majorcan's behaviour be regarded as servility? Unamuno does not think so, maintaining that Majorcans had no need to be servile in a country where poverty and unemployment do not exist. If a Majorcan "knows his place", that is a result of the intensely conservative tradition by which the lives of the islanders are ruled. People are called by God to a certain state of life and for each state of life there is a well-established rule of conduct towards other states both higher and more lowly, with which all Majorcans are perfectly familiar. The Majorcan is in fact imbued with that spirit of civil subordination for which Doctor Johnson prided himself on being "so zealous". It is a spirit which is, of course, highly satisfactory for those who are set in authority but it may be questioned whether it does not lead to a certain intellectual dullness and staleness or even to political supineness. One eminent Majorcan has complained that this has indeed been the result and the particular Majorcan characteristic of "rancidness", which incorporates all these defects, has been noted by more than one foreign observer.

However, no one could have accused Francisca of being rancid, for all the deference she showed her temporary employers. So robust a character made you try to earn her deference. Her manners were the kind that would beget good manners where she did not already find them. She was the sort of person who would stand no nonsense, particularly from other servants or the trades people, to use an old-fashioned term suitable to the context. She would not tolerate impertinence from younger people and she was apt to be impatient with other members of our household who worked less hard than herself. She appeared to take it as a personal affront when we were overcharged by the shops and constantly urged us not to stand nonsense of that sort.

In her efforts to keep house for us as economically as possible she did not hesitate to employ the services of her husband, Fernando. An old soldier with the name and the manner of a conquistador, he lived by himself in Puerto Pollensa except when Francisca was able to join him on her days off. Unlike her, he did not work very hard, though they had nearly an acre of good land to cultivate. After a day's restful gardening Fernando usually found it necessary to take a day's holiday and he had therefore plenty of opportunity to investigate local prices, upon which, according to Francisca, he was an authority.

George Sand loathed the food she had had in Majorca and years after, when the bad taste ought to have left her palate and the bad smell her nostrils, she wrote of it with disgust. This disgust was no doubt due partly to an admittedly disagreeable experience: "One day when a thin chicken was brought in, we saw jumping on its smoking back some enormous Master Fleas, which Hoffman would have turned into evil spirits, but which he would certainly have not eaten in gravy." No such eccentric recipe - "poulet à la puce" perhaps or "fleas on chicken back" - figured in Francisca's repertoire, which was extensive and varied. Moreover she was able to make delicious dishes out of comparatively cheap and ordinary materials, and in this she showed her genius as a cook. The staple ingredients of most of her cooking for us were the magnificent vegetables which are grown locally and in profusion. Artichokes, broad beans, chick peas, lentils and French beans, but above all artichokes, she would combine with each other or with meat or fish and subject to a myriad different culinary processes, for which the locally made olive oil was indispensable. George Sand was vehement in her denunciation of Majorcan olive oil, but either she exaggerated its badness or it has improved considerably since her day. There are of course a number of different qualities, from the most expensive at 30 pesetas a litre to the cheapest at 10 pesetas (N.B. at 1955 prices). We found the "corriente" at 14.50 pesetas perfectly agreeable, and its faintly unrefined tang seemed appropriate to the peasant food, which was our daily fare. Sometimes the smell of it would pervade the house and remind us, if we needed reminding, that we were in Spain as well as Majorca.

One of Francisca's most popular creations was a kind of vegetable mould known as Granada. Its ingredients are eggs, oil and as many different kinds of vegetables as you have. It is baked in the oven and you eat it like a cake, which made it a convenient food for picnics. The eggs, which were laid locally by chickens kept in the courtyards of Pollensa houses, were delicious. We had them every morning fried in "corriente" oil and even our most British stomachs did not fail to be charmed. One member of the party, in a fine initial flush of enthusiasm for the principle of doing in Rome what the Romans do, ate at first bread and salt and nothing else for breakfast but very soon succumbed to the enticement of other people's fried eggs.

The Englishman's preference for tasteless emasculated white bread appears to have become known in Majorca for Francisca at first procured loaves of this especially for us, insisting that the "pan corriente" would positively not be agreeable to our sensitive civilized palates. We eventually prevailed upon her to allow us to try it and found, as we had expected, that it was excellent. It was also considerably cheaper than the white.

Fish was another staple of our diet and particularly a certain shark-like fish which we later discovered to be a lamprey. One of these usually provided three meals, its roe for luncheon, part of it fried for dinner and the remainder "soused" for supper, when Francisca was out. Squid too made its appearance frequently at the table, rather too frequently in fact for Henry Yorke (the novelist Henry Green), who made no bones about his detestation of a creature which, he alleged, lived on drowned sailors. But Francisca had a nephew, who when off duty from the Hotel would go fishing in the Bay, and the product from these expeditions was duly brought up to the Villa for profitable disposal.

Snails were also a less popular dish. One day Francisca, at our request it must be admitted, produced a small washing basket filled with the most gigantic molluscs. We looked at them with admiration tinged slightly perhaps with apprehension. In due course they or at least some of them appeared smoking on the table, accompanied by a dish of mayonnaise sauce. I did not then know and I doubt if Francisca knew that mayonnaise originated in the Balearics, having been invented by the French garrison of Mahon during the French occupation of Minorca (1756-1763), when local olive oil was substituted for scarce butter. For many if not most snail eaters, if the truth were known, the chief and perhaps sole attraction of snails, indeed the means that make them at all palatable, is the parsley and garlic butter, with which the French market them all over the world. We were therefore dismayed, when it became apparent to us that mayonnaise sauce was being offered by Francisca as an adequate substitute, which it most emphatically was not. Nor, I fear, were Francisca's other attempts at "selling" us these leathery molluscs any more successful,* even when she served them without their shells in a sort of stew, a disguise which did not fool our most fervent opponent of the horrid practice of snail eating. They were, it seems, at one time considered a rare delicacy in the ancient and "rancid" city of Alcudia, but we were not tempted to investigate this particular piece of local lore.

For sweetness there was ambrosial Pollensa honey, redolent of the aromatic shrubs, but particularly of the myrtle, that grow on the hillsides of Pollensa and Formentor, whose very names seemed to evoke a land flowing with milk and honey. But the milk did not come from the neighbourhood and not so long ago it was virtually unobtainable in Majorca. The islanders do not in fact

*Elizabeth Carter gives in her *Majorcan Food and Cookery* (Prospect Books 1989) several Majorcan methods of preparing snails.

have much use for the cow, which is expensive to keep in a country where there is very little pasture land. George Sand bitterly lamented the lack of butter and even today it is of an inferior quality (though it may have improved since 1955). The cheese on the other hand, made from goat's milk, pungent and smoky, was delicious.

For sweetness there were two other local products. One afternoon we discovered Francisca and Madalena busily cutting away the viciously thorny leaves from a pile of palmetto tufts. They offered us some of the whitish roots laid bare by their treatment and we accepted somewhat doubtfully. We found them sweet and refreshing, but hardly worth the labour of preparation.

Whoever was the first to suggest that the Gardens of the Hesperides were to be found in Majorca must certainly have eaten a Pollensa orange. This divine fruit, made for a god's dessert, also became ours soon after our arrival at Formentor. We had never tasted any fruit more delectable; not even a Siamese mango or an English peach could surpass it in flavour and texture. Golden as a sovereign, larger than a grapefruit but not so perfectly spherical, the Pollensa orange has no pulp and its juice when you eat it seems to be crushed as from gossamer and floods the mouth like ripe grapes filling the flushed cheeks of a rococo Bacchus. The Soller orange is better known and has been exported to England but it is not as good as the rich and rare product of the Pollensa valley,* whose season is all too soon over. At the beginning of April we bought them at four pesetas the kilo, but soon the price rose fifty cents a day until Pollensa oranges cost twice as much a kilo as Valencian oranges, and since they also weigh twice as much it meant that for a Pollensa orange, you would have to pay four times as much as for a Valencian. When this point was reached Pollensa oranges disappeared from the market.

In Majorca in the spring, though the days are hot, the evenings are chilly enough for a fire to be a comfort. The evening fire was responsible for our only chore, if such a term (suggesting as it does greasy dishes and soot-blackened hearths) may properly be employed for the pleasant task of collecting sticks and fir cones from the woods. We did this, as it seemed the only possible way open to us to economise our small stock of pesetas. Moreover a little productive labour added flavour to our daily dish of idleness, especially as we enjoyed the fruits of it when idleness was brought to the point of perfection after a good dinner.

Wood collecting soon gave rise to a healthy spirit of capitalist competition or perhaps socialist emulation among the members of the party: bigger and better cones, longer and fatter sticks were produced by the foragers, who were obliged to go farther afield as the immediate confines of the Villa were scoured clean. Since there were no controls, nor inspectors to enforce them if there had been, certain abuses grew up in the industry and a number of undesirable practices were introduced by the sharper operators, who at our evening sessions around the fire would frequently add to the sense of injury, provoked by their dubious methods of collection, the insult of a preposterous claim to other more socially-minded persons' lawfully acquired sticks.

For our Majorcan Nights' Entertainment we could also often depend on the story-telling genius of Henry whose novelist's delight in the idiocies and idiocyncrasies of the people he knows was as infectious as the gaiety of his wife. "Aunt Yorke" to our three year old son, she diffused the glamour of the '20's,

* Mrs Boyd in 1911 bought large golden oranges at Pollensa at 2d a dozen.

authentic and undiminished. Their adventures on their way to join us at the Villa formed the subject of one of Henry's best stories, as it did also years later for his television play. Things had begun to go badly wrong at Barcelona which they reached on Good Friday in the afternoon, by which time their tickets for the Palma boat were no longer valid. Their travel agency in London had not apparently been aware or had forgotten to warn them of the eccentric and quite inexplicable rule of the Transmediterranea Company by which, if a reservation is not claimed by mid-day of the sailing date, it is automatically cancelled. It was, therefore, to say the least, a serious "choc psychologique" when, on arriving at the Company's offices, which they reached laboriously by tram, there being no taxis on account of the fiesta, they were informed that it would be quite impossible for them to sail that night.

Confronted by this categorical non-possumus, they were put on their mettle and determined that they would, come what may, embark for Palma that night. Henry, having considerable, if in this instance misplaced, confidence in the influence and ingenuity of the hall porters of the most expensive hotels decided to turn for assistance to a promising member of the corps. The man was a disappointment however, a blimp it would seem among commissionaires, devoid of any scheme or artifice with which to extricate travellers stranded on a Good Friday.

It was a character at a bar who eventually delivered the goods - they very often do - and after a number of obscure and tortuous transactions in which several other characters were involved, Henry and his gallant travelling companion were hustled on board the steamer like a couple of illegal immigrants, in which rôle they seem to have stayed until the end of the voyage. The Novelist, distinguished indeed to the literary public but incognito to an unliterary and very possibly illiterate steward, was locked like the old lady in a spotlessly clean lavatory, where he spent the night with his head not over but under a basin. His wife fared better and was provided by a chivalrous attendant with a mattress and a few square feet of steerage. When we met them the next morning looking wanly over Palma Bay from the terrace of another most expensive hotel, it was clear that they were still suffering from the "choc psychologique" of the previous day, which their subsequent experiences as stowaways had rather naturally failed to soothe.

Another distinguished novelist has also told the story of a similarly uncomfortable experience on the Palma boat, but with much less humour. George Sand complains bitterly in "Un Hiver à Majorque" of the treatment accorded to passengers by the captain of the boat, "un petit vapeur anglais", in which she and Chopin and the children returned to Barcelona. She too had the key turned on her but she was at least in her cabin, not in a lavatory.

We were more fortunate and both our crossings were made in great comfort, though on our return voyage a number of formalities had to be carried out with the assistance of a stout stewardess before two matrimonial couples, temporarily separated by an unfeeling shipping company, could be re-united in two matrimonial cabins. It must be said too that the arrangements at Barcelona for putting a tourist's car on board leave something to be desired.*

I had to wait for hours while bananas were being loaded - pigs took precedence over George Sand. While I was waiting I talked to a Minorcan, who told me of the traces of the English still to be observed in his island. He seemed to

*In 1954 cars were hoisted on board by a derrick and lowered into a hold.

regard the English with affection, contrary to what a recent Spanish pamphlet about Minorca had led me to expect. His conversation was a welcome diversion as I shivered on the quay while cartloads of bananas from the Canaries were dumped endlessly into the hold of the "Ciudad de Palma".

Both Henry and his audience, while stories were being told, were encouraged by libations of vino tinto, as the Spaniards so aptly call that inky red wine of the country. But after a time the combined effects of alcohol, sea and sunshine would prove too strong for further intellectual effort and with the aromatic scent of burning pinewood in our nostrils we would totter sleepily off to bed.

The comparative cheapness of alcohol is of course one of the major attractions of the Continent and it is not by any means the least of the charms of the Greater Aphrodisiad. Vino tinto cost four pesetas a litre (in 1955) at the Puerto and three and a half pesetas a litre if we bought it from one of the cool wine shops at Pollensa. It was even cheaper at Inca but though the wine of Binisalem, which is sold there is generally reckoned superior to the red wine from other parts of Majorca, we preferred our local produce. In the hot weather Vino Tinto is perhaps a little too heavy and we used therefore to drink the Vin Rosé which came unadulterated from the farmer and which we bought at two pesetas fifty from a wine shop at Alcudia.

On special occasions we would sample a bottle of Majorcan champagne which, as we had no ice, we would cool by suspending the bottle in the well or reservoir underneath the house. I must reluctantly confess however that our experiments in local champagne were not entirely successful, and though there may well be some Majorcan vintages that would stand comparison with the produce of Rheims we never had the good fortune to taste anything that was as good as champagne cider.

Majorcan gin too was disappointing, though very cheap. It had a pungent flavour which, while not exactly offensive, was too strong to be drowned by anything with which it was mixed. We stuck to Spanish brands which were closely and successfully modelled on a well known British product even to the shape of the bottle. When the cellar at the Villa was empty, as it occasionally became, or when we felt we needed to renew our acquaintance with the world, we would descend to the Hotel.

There are not, I suppose, many hotels where you will find in the garden a marble bust of the founder. But the founder of the Hotel Formentor was himself exceptional. Born in the Argentine, Adán Diehl came to Majorca and settled in Pollensa in whose artistic circles he soon became prominent. Yet artist though he was, he felt an irresistible inclination towards the hotel business, no doubt inherited from his Spanish ancestors, and in 1928 he conceived the idea of throwing open to the world, or at least to the world's elite, the hitherto inviolate beauties of Formentor Bay. It was a project that found considerable support among his friends in Majorca and a company was soon formed to put it into effect.

The whole of the Formentor Peninsula was acquired by the Company and the present motor road was built from Puerto Pollensa, so that for the first time the valley was made accessible to vehicular traffic. A sentimentalist, who visited Formentor Bay about this time, lamented that many of the "gigantic pine trees had recently alas been cut down". Yet in the siting and design of his hotel Diehl showed that he was indeed an artist and that the noble pines had not been felled in vain. Only the most uncompromising tree lover, the most misanthropic of backwoodsmen could surely object to so discreet an intrusion upon Formentor's age long seclusion. The long white building, which was completed in 1930, is bounded on three sides by the forest but the land in front has been cleared to some extent to make room for a broad terrace and below it a magnificent garden. From the terrace a wide flight of steps inspired, almost certainly, by the ascent to the Calvario at Pollensa, leads down through the garden to the little stone jetty where tourists and the provisions from Pollensa are unloaded.

In its early days the Hotel included among its patrons many distinguished people, such as the Prince of Wales, Winston Churchill, and the Chinese film star Anna May Wong. The Spanish writer José Maria Salaverria described in his *Viaje a Mallorca* (1933) - a sort of counterblast to George Sand's *Voyage à Majorque* - a visit to Formentor. He was invited by Diehl to a drinks party to meet some of the more intellectual of the Hotel's guests. Afterwards Diehl took him on a tour of the Peninsula and showed him a cove, a *calita*, where he planned to found a colony of poets and painters. This had been his dream when he first saw Formentor but he succeeded hitherto only in creating a refuge for millionaires. He never did realise his dream and the man, who assured Salaverria that he was not a captain of industry but a dabbler in Argentinian politics and a frequenter of Paris salons, lost his entire fortune in the Hotel and returned to Argentina, where he died in 1953. Ruin was also the fate of another foreigner rash enough to launch a great enterprise in the vicinity of Formentor and it seems that Majorca does not take kindly to development, however enlightened, by others than natives of the island, in which perhaps there is much wisdom and to which also much of the people's happiness as well as the "staleness" noted by D. H. Lawrence should be attributed.

In 1954 the owners of the Hotel, all of whom were Majorcan, inheritors of Diehl's inspired creation, were better businessmen and succeeded where he failed, in making it profitable. In doing so they have also made it the means of preserving the Formentor peninsula for the enjoyment of all who could get to it,* at the same time giving useful and lucrative employment to more than two hundred people of the neighbourhood. Only two or three members of the hotel staff were not Majorcans and most of them came from Pollensa or the Puerto. Even the band, which played with immense and cheerful zest, came, to a man and a girl, from the town of Inca; a fact of which everybody was very proud. For the greater comfort of the Hotel guests a stretch of sand was regularly raked smooth and free of anything offensive to foot or eye. One morning when we were lying, not in this privileged arena but upon our customary patch of unraked sand, we were startled by the approach of an extraordinary figure wearing white shorts and a Bavarian hat and brandishing an alpenstock. He was accompanied in his mountainous progress across the sands by one of those homely looking women whose clothes seemed to have shrivelled with their figures. This couple belonged to the German brigade, which at times was prominent if not obtrusive at Formentor. Members of it could be heard moving gutturally about the groves or making ponderous splashings in the sea, spasmodically submerging like so many pocket submarines. Once we saw a carload of them, all male, dashing off to the light-

---

*In spite of a small cafeteria which has been built among the pines bordering the sands, this was still true in 1990.

house in a cloud of dust, bound no doubt for a clandestine rendez-vous on a lonely part of the coast, as someone suggested. Henry added point to the suggestion, when he told us that the last or penultimate 'plane out of the Berlin Bunker had flown direct to Formentor and this story, though I have since failed to confirm it, increased our mock suspicion that Formentor might be a hotbed of Teutonic intrigue. Sinister speculations of a similar nature were further nourished when we heard of the local rumour that Italian officers had been seen at the seaplane base at the Puerto.

The American contingent was also important though in constant need of reinforcement as casualties were heavy. The Americans preferred as a rule to rush in for a day or two, time to despatch a picture postcard of the "most beautiful spot in the world", and then move on as quickly as possible to the next letter box.

The British on the other hand were better hotel guests. They came for a fortnight or three weeks or for as long as their foreign currency would allow. As a result, I suppose, their tastes were given particular consideration, their palates most favoured nation's treatment and the cuisine had distinct affinities with the version of continental fare offered by our larger seaside hotels.

During the Easter holiday the Anglo-Saxon element was drowned in a flood of Iberians who arrived *en bloc* from Barcelona in an Italian liner, which anchored in Formentor Bay and provided a pleasant addition to our landscape from the terrace. We did not see much of the passengers however, who having disembarked, remained on board, as it were, at the hotel and after a few days departed leaving the Bay empty as before.

Before World War II the British Mediterranean Fleet used to visit Pollensa Bay, whose shores, according to popular legend, then reverberated with exploding champagne corks. These naval picnics have not been repeated since the Spanish Civil War, though the White Ensign did once show itself discreetly in the Bay, while we were there, when a member of "The Royal Yacht Squadron" paid a dignified call. Other craft, equally sumptuous but of less social standing, also occasionally anchored off shore. These aspired only to a Blue Ensign and whereas "The Squadron" took its ease on deck decorously in a deck chair, the auxiliary vessels sprawled in abandoned attitudes on lilos.

The heirs and successors of Adán Diehl fully maintained the standard of good taste which he originally set and nothing was permitted at Formentor to detract from its natural beauty. Any artificial additions to the landscape were made to blend with it. Even the beach umbrellas, which during the summer months afforded necessary shade to the sun-worshippers, were made locally and from local materials. Their manufacture was an annual event for the beach staff who, under the direction of the skipper of the launch that brought our provisions, got busy one morning in May with wire and dried rushes. They lacked practice at the work however and many were the failures and powerful were the imprecations before a finished article was set up on the sands to look like an outsize version of the hat generally worn in illustrations of Robinson Crusoe.

On most days all of us would walk down through the pine trees to the white rim of the bay - all of us that is except Henry, who refused to budge from the Villa, though he was once enticed from it by reports of something extra special in Bikinis. As a rule he preferred to remain on the terrace, sipping Vino Tinto, baking his face a dull rust colour and losing himself in the wide open pages of "Arabia Deserta". That was his story, or part of it. There were also his frequent expressions of admiration for the way Madalena sang while she worked upstairs - to him, so he claimed, though with what justification and with what effect we never could discover. In the cool of the evening he would leave the terrace and saunter off in search of his quota of firewood. He did not, like the rest of us, have to go far from the Villa. While we rootled laboriously in the undergrowth, Henry with magnificent ruthlessness filched thick sticks and thin logs from the woodsmen's stacks at the side of the road. In this he was aided and abetted by his Senora who kept 'cave' as seriously as any schoolboy. Henry's wood collecting ardour suffered a temporary cooling when the news filtered through to the Villa that Chelsea had won a victory. Such was his football fan's elation that he declared roundly that from then on he was not going to do a stroke. Happily he was not as good as his word and we continued to benefit from his exertions, though at the woodsmen's expense.

They were our nearest neighbours, for when they were not busy ten hours a day felling and cutting up trees, they lived in a kind of rustic barrack room just below the Villa. There they slept and cooked their meals, each man having his own rough brick fireplace in a penthouse adjoining the barrack. Some evenings after it was dark we could discern through the trees the flicker of flames from their woodland bivouac while the sound of bass voices, borne on the tranquil air, would breach intermittently the seclusion of our retreat. Varying in intensity like the light of the fire, they would at one moment blaze into robust laughter, at another die away into a hushed murmur, as an eager audience paid attention to some tale. But these infrequent revelries did not last long, for sleep soon overcame the woodsmen after their hard day's work among the pines; both flames and laughter would be extinguished and only the nightingale would then disturb the profound silence of the valley.

I suspect that woodsmen are a shy race, perhaps from the nature of their calling. Since most of their lives are passed in the loneliness of a forest and often remote from towns and villages, they must subconsciously lose the need for and habit of social intercourse, finding adequate human companionship among their fellow workers and perhaps too some kind of spiritual satisfaction from their constant contact with the life of the woods - though this may be pure romantic speculation on the part of one to whom the forest is not a source of livelihood. At all events we never got to know our neighbours and when we met them, as we sometimes did along the road or on a forest path, their greetings never extended to more than an absent-minded grunt.

One afternoon I attempted unsuccessfully to penetrate this reserve. I came across a team of three working on a large tree, which had recently been felled. One man was lopping off branches with an axe shaped like a tomahawk and the other two were sawing the trunk into five feet lengths with a cross cut saw. I asked if I might take a turn with it. They looked at me curiously and perhaps a little doubtfully, but politely invited me to try. One of them surrendered his end of the saw to me and work was resumed in silence. My efforts at conversation were shyly received and I very soon felt that if I was not exactly an intruder, my departure would not be regretted. So I thanked them for letting me "have a go" and took myself off, but not before my temporary mate had told me that he could see that I had "worked", a compliment which I value highly.

At last the time came early one morning to leave our sanctuary among the pines and to say farewell to our guardian angel Francisca. She helped us stack the luggage in the car (it was a 1923 Silver Ghost open tourer; the body was described as "Torpedo" shaped and it was painted battleship grey) up to its gunwales and, amid tears and much waving of handkerchiefs, we drove away from the Villa for the last time. Slowly we wound our way up the steep road to the pass of Mal Pas and as we neared the summit we paused to look back and take a last impression of the happy valley. A slight haze seemed to tinge the trees with silver but the mountain tops and the Bay were soaked in the purple of a most glorious dawn, such as might have inspired Rubén Darío's famous stanza:

*Juventud divino tesoro*
*Ya te vas para no volver*
*Quando quiero llorar no lloro*
*Y a veces lloro sin querer*

*Mas es mia el alba de oro.*

Youth divine treasure
Now thou leavest never to return
When I wish to weep I do not weep
And sometimes I weep, when I do not wish

Yet mine is the dawn of gold.

# CHAPTER II
## THE NEIGHBOURING COUNTRY

The day after our arrival at the Villa we climbed the hill behind and, emerging onto a clearing among the pine trees strewn with rocks and grey boulders, we suddenly saw stretched below us the valley of Formentor. It was not Erewhon, nor the land of King Solomon's Mines, nor the vale of Lombardy, but our sensations of surprise and delight must have been akin to those experienced by the heroes of Samuel Butler and Rider Haggard and by the Army of Italy on first catching sight of their enchanted valleys. Unlike these, however, the valley of Formentor is not particularly fertile in spite of its name, and the only sign of cultivation was a patch of light green in the midst of a dark forest of pine trees. Its enchantment is due chiefly to its being isolated from the world by the steep mountains which enclose it on every side except for three small gaps at Formentor itself, at Cala Figueras and at Cala Murta.*

As we looked down upon it on that April morning from our precipitous vantage point, we could not see these gaps and the valley appeared to be inviolate. A deep peace reigned over it and the single dwelling place visible near the patch of cultivation, looked as if it should be occupied by the Three Bears. One day we visited this house and the fairy tale atmosphere with which we had invested it was soon dispelled by the sight of bleeding corpses of silly sheep in the process of being skinned.

The former seat of the Lords of Formentor, the Casas Velles (Old Houses), as it is known locally, is indeed very ancient, though a part of it dates from the nineteenth century. It was occupied only by the labourers who look after the farm, which supplied the Hotel with eggs and other produce. They showed us the living room and the kitchen of the original dwelling, with its white-washed walls hung with antediluvian fire-arms, and its massive front door scarred, according to legend, by the bullets of Moorish marauders. I enquired if they got any shooting now, "No, it is not permitted," they said, and in any case there was not much game to shoot, only rabbits. There can scarely have been many of these for we never saw one, though there were traces of them, traces which never ceased to interest a three year old member of the party, who was perfectly oblivious to the scenery etc which enthralled his elders and betters.

Rabbits were not always so scarce in Majorca and the Cabo Conejo (rabbit), the name of one of the headlands on the eastern side of the Formentor peninsula, suggests that they must once have been plentiful. Certainly they were in Roman days when Formentor was golden with wheat (*frumentum*) and when the inhabitants of Majorca were as much afflicted by rabbits as the farmers of England and France were before modern methods of extermination came to their help. The situation in Majorca became so serious in the reign of the Emperor Augustus that the islanders "dispatced an embassy to the Senate, requesting succour against the rabbits, which having multiplied to an excessive number destroyed the corn, plants and trees and would not suffer them to live in quiet in these islands [the Baleares]. They begged to have other lands to inhabit because these animals had driven them out of their houses."

What if anything the Senate did about this petition, the historian does not relate. It is unlikely that they were able to arrange for a mass evacuation of the

*Cala (French, *Escale*, a port of call, from the Arabic *Kalla*, a place protected from the wind, a harbour) is a small inlet on the coast.

population to another part of the Empire. What does seem probable is that another animal was introduced into the islands to prey upon the rabbits. Certainly wild cats formerly abounded and these fierce creatures would have been effective as rabbit destroyers. But they too have almost disappeared, so relentlessly have they been trapped and shot by local sportsmen. According to George Sand the skin of this animal was used to make the hats worn by Majorcan men, and this no doubt was one of the chief reasons why it has become so scarce. The woodsmen of Formentor still set traps for it hopefully but, I believe, vainly. One such trap was always to be seen - empty - near the path which led from the Villa to the sea-shore. It was a simple affair, being a plain oblong wooden box with a door which theoretically would drop if any animal should be so foolish as to enter it. At the Puerto there was a stuffed wild cat at the cake shop and that was the only one we ever saw, though Henry alleged he had seen the eyes of one gleaming in the woods at night, on his return from a visit to the Hotel in search of Fundador, his favourite brand of Spanish brandy. The allegation, whether founded on fact or on Fundador, was avowedly made to make our flesh creep, for a wild cat, if the one at the confectioner's was a fair specimen of the breed, would not have been a cosy pet to meet on a dark night. Its small head seemed to have no other purpose than to provide a magazine for two rows of razor sharp teeth, and such was the impression of ferocity they gave, that even its glass eyes seemed positively to stare at one with a wicked about-to-pounce glint. Its long thin body was arched as if ready to spring and fasten its talon-like claws in a mesmerised prey. Clearly an animal that would make any rabbit's flesh creep.

There was one other farm in the valley of Formentor situated at the entrance to one of the gaps in the ring of mountains at Cala Murta. I walked to it one afternoon along the dusty road which bisects the valley and leads ultimately to the lighthouse. At the end of the valley, just before the road disappears into a tunnel beneath the rock face of the mountain called Fumat, there is a pathway to the right which skirts the farm and winds down to the sea. I turned into it and walked first through pine trees and then through thick groves of sombre ilex. The sky above the narrow pathway was dark with storm clouds and I was enveloped in a hushed solitude. Oppressed by the utter silence I began to walk a little faster, when suddenly there was a crashing in the undergrowth and I saw on the other side of a dried up bed of a torrent, two black horses. They must certainly be wild ones, possibly even apocalyptic, I thought agitatedly and hurried on. Soon afterwards I emerged from the ilex wood and found myself on the beach, where a couple were having a picnic. I had had enough of romantic solitude and was quite glad to see them and their yellow car.

The Cala Murta or Myrtle Cove is a small rocky inlet, hemmed in by the mountain sides and with a narrow opening to Pollensa Bay. Nature by her combination of trees, rocks and sea has made it a beautiful place and man, perhaps unconsciously, has succeeded in further embellishing it. At one end of the narrow beach there is a wall of granite, which forms a succession of terraces up the mountain side. It is made of large blocks of different shapes, but so perfectly fitted together that it is impossible to insert the blade of a pocket-knife between them, while the top outer edge is a smooth straight line without the smallest indentation. It was not immediately apparent what the purpose of this exquisite piece of stonework was and I assumed it was part of some scheme recently abandoned. I was quite wrong and some weeks later discovered from a local expert that it had been built "when there was a Queen in Spain". It was in fact the seaward end of the pathway, which had been constructed from Cala Murta to Cape Formentor when the lighthouse was built in 1862 in the reign of Queen Isabella, and which was the only means of approach to it until the motor road was completed a few years ago.

It was at Cala Murta that Diehl hoped to found his colony of poets and painters. When asked by Diehl what he thought of it, Salaverria replied in terms which burst even his bounds of eloquence in praise of Mallorca. "Incomparable. Here one feels so far from the world, so enclosed by the island and so deep in a desert, which the most solemn beauty sanctifies, that one would want to return to the innocent life of a primitive fisherman."

On my homeward walk I stopped at the farm house. Near the entrance in a penthouse I found a very old man and a sullen looking boy, crouched over a heap of palmetto shoots which they were preparing for eating. I explained to the old man, who evidently had little Spanish, at any rate of the kind I spoke, that I wished to visit the chapel. He eventually understood me and told the boy to show it to me. I followed him into the courtyard round which the farmhouse was built, and passing under a large fig tree, entered by a doorway into an immaculately clean passage way, which gave access to the chapel. This I found disappointing. It was by any standard grossly overloaded with cruci-fixes and it was decorated with gaudy Romanesque murals, depicting the Majorcan saints Raymond Lull, Catalina Tomas and Fray Junípero Serra.*

There was a small harmonium and a red plush priedieu, upon which I knelt while the boy, exhausted with ennui, leaned disdainfully against the door. When I rose to leave, I observed a framed notice hanging on the wall. It was signed by the Bishop of Palma, who promised indulgences to anyone who said a certain number of prayers for a hundred days in the Chapel petitioning for peace among Christian Princes and the extirpation of heretics. I left the building with the hope that the prayers for the latter object would be few and ineffective, and reflecting that prayers for the former, in view of the strictly limited number of Christian monarchs, would scarcely be very useful.

Having said good-bye to the old man, I was just in time to hail the yellow car as it came bumping up the path and the couple kindly invited me to "jump in". As we drove back along the lighthouse road, I had the satisfaction of being asked by the driver, who looked like an Arab, "Did you see those wild horses?"

We became quite familiar with that road after several trips to the lighthouse. Most people, I imagine, have some sort of feeling for lighthouses, whether of curiosity or romance or, even, as one eccentric once revealed to me at an ambassadorial luncheon table, of primitive and amused reverence for their traditional shape. By their close association with the ceaseless drama of the sea, by their often spectacular or isolated situation and by the very nature of their task and the equipment used for it, lighthouses must surely always exer-cise a certain fascination and it is not difficult to understand why Sir Winston Churchill should have apparently derived such satisfaction from being an Elder Brother of Trinity House.

The lighthouse of Cape Formentor can have few rivals from any point of view. It is approached by a road that is not only of quite stupendous scenic

* Raymond Lull and Fray Junípero have not been canonised, though they have been strongly recommended.

magnificence but which is also an engineering triumph. It climbs steeply from the valley of Formentor, hewn out of the mountain side far above the fjord of Cala Figuera, pierces Mount Fumat by a rock tunnel and then winds among and around the bare rock summits of the Formentor headland affording vertiginous glimpses of the sea and suddenly and dramatically revealing the lighthouse.

Built nearly a century ago on the top of a sheer rock cliff some 600 feet high, the lighthouse is a lonely and most impressive monument to human endeavour. Its loneliness has however been mitigated since the construction of the motor road and its two guardians and their families, who share a car, seemed quite contented with their lot and, as they were natives of Pollensa, were unwilling to exchange their isolated and, in winter, storm battered lighthouse for a more civilised one further from home. The motor car suggested that the profession of lighthouse keeper had become more respectable since the days of Queen Isabella and this was confirmed when I was told the Spanish for "lighthouse keeper". It used to be plain "Torrero", but just as in English an "undertaker" is now rarely anything less than a "funeral director" so the Spanish lighthouse keeper has graduated to a "Técnico Mecánico de los Señales Marítimos".

The round tower that crowns the mountain enclosing the landward end of the Formentor peninsula was built for a purpose diametrically opposite to that of the lighthouse and the difference in purpose explains the difference in site. Whereas the lighthouse is situated as near to the sea as possible in order to warn seafarers of the dangers from the land, the tower was placed as far inland as possible in order to warn the landsmen of the dangers from the sea. The tower or Atalaya of Formentor was built towards the end of the sixteenth century by the University of Majorca and like the many similar towers that were erected on commanding points around the coast of Majorca, was designed to warn the inhabitants of the approach of Moorish invaders, who continually afflicted the islanders until the beginning of the nineteenth century.*

We walked up to it one afternoon, for there is a motor road which winds up the mountain side almost to the base of the tower and we were well rewarded for our trouble. With one exception the mountain or hill of Albercuitx (390 metres) is the highest point on the Formentor peninsula and it might have been designed specially by the Creator to support a watch tower. From its summit we could see southwards over the whole of Pollensa and Alcudia Bays, northwards and eastwards over the whole of the Formentor peninsula and to the sea beyond. Only the highest peaks would have interrupted the seaward gaze of an anxious coastguard. We found, rather to our surprise, a soldier filling that role with obvious inadequacy. He was clearly pleased to see us and I have no doubt that this was because a visit from almost any human being was welcome to one whose vigil was not merely lonely, but really unnecessary. He invited me to climb the rungs which formed a ladder up the wall of the tower to an aperture about twenty feet above the ground and the only means of ingress. Having climbed through it I found myself in a circular room with a domed ceiling covered with coloured drawings of German and Allied aircraft, relics of the wartime use of the tower by air-watchers. A further series of rungs and a narrow hole gave access to the crenellated roof on

*The last raid on Deyá was in 1820.

which a battered sentry box stood. I leant over an embrasure, whose great thickness failed to reassure me, as I looked dizzily down about a thousand feet to the sea almost immediately below. I drew back with a start when I suddenly heard a footstep behind me. The soldier had followed me up and was evidently amused at my nervousness. We surveyed the landscape together while he told me alternately about his life and the surrounding landmarks; the tower capped promontory of Victoria, the distant outline of the Puig Major, the highest mountain in Majorca, the tower known as the Castillo del Rey and the two most notable peaks of the Formentor peninsula, El Pal and the Falda de na Blanca, or the 'Skirt of Lady Blanca'.

We had already been to the top of the latter for, though it looks formidable, its ascent is literally child's play, having been accomplished by one of the younger members of our party, aged three. As a walk it is counted among the attractions of the Hotel and with reason, for it would be difficult for the patrons of such establishments to find a more satisfactory combination of easy accessibility with precipitous grandeur. It was a delight for the senses to walk along this mountain path, breathing the scent of aromatic shrubs, catching glimpses of asphodels, wild freesias and cyclamen, and observing the panorama of mountain and sea and forest changing as the path wound gradually upwards. At the top, which is a bare rock-strewn plateau, there is a circle of masonry, presumably all that is left of a former watch tower. There is, or was, also a flock of goats, reputedly wild, which hop dangerously along the skyline, peeping at the two legged intruders as if hoping to see one of them sprain an ankle.

As for El Pal, though his name exercised and no doubt overstrained our wit, we never succeeded in getting to his summit, for this involves more than a mere walk. His sides are steep and very rough and though he is only some 1,400 feet high, he seemed a good deal higher when we tried to find our own way up without the help of a guide or recognisable track. We never got beyond one of his shoulders and there abandoned the attempt.

Another upland expedition was more successful. Though everybody knew that there was nothing but the sea beyond, I had nevertheless felt an urge to climb to the rim of the Formentor valley and look over it and see for myself. Aiming at a place where it was lowest, several of us set off one afternoon from the lighthouse road. We followed a track through the pine woods, which took us past a clearing where there was considerable building activity. We stopped to watch it. There were a number of distinct but closely related operations of which the most important and the one upon which the others depended was the quarrying of sandstone by methods that can have altered little, if at all, since the days of the Romans. The stone was being cut out of the ground in flat rectangular slabs by an old man chipping with a kind of pickaxe. He was working round the edges of a slab and since no other implement was visible, presumably it was also used for detaching the underside of the slab from the quarry, though it was not easy to imagine how. The quarry, a rectangular hole, was already over ten feet deep and the slabs were being hoisted up out of it by means of a crude windlass, made of branches and pieces of old rope. It was being operated by a youth whose rustic features matched his machine. I asked if I might work it and, permission being given, I hauled up a load of slabs, but when it had reached the level of the ground, the youth was instructed to take over, for the final stage of the operation involved swinging the load inwards and on to the ground and at the same time letting go the winch. Clearly it was not thought that a stranger could be capable of executing this manoeuvre satisfactorily and it would certainly have gone hard with the old man chipping below if he wasn't.

Once the quarry had reached a certain size it was abandoned as a source of stone and converted into a covered reservoir. Several such quarries were already being roofed with recently cut stone.

Also watching the workmen was a swarthy man in a beret, who was to be seen in different parts of the Formentor estate, wherever work was in progress, looking on grimly and silently. He had a motor cycle on which he rushed sputteringly from the scene of one operation to another. I discovered that he was one of the owners of the Hotel and that his main task was to act as overseer and ensure that there was no slacking by the Hotel estate workers. It is apparently a characteristic of Majorcan workers that they work better under the eye of such an overseer.

Beyond the quarries the valley narrowed and soon we were walking up a steep pathway that followed the bottom of the fold in the mountain. At intervals we passed circular raised platforms, whose purpose was not immediately apparent. They had evidently long been disused, long enough perhaps, we speculated ignorantly, to have some connexion with the mysterious prehistoric dwellings or burial places known as clapotes in which the neighbourhood of Formentor abounds.

Had they conceivably been designed for the celebration of some Druidical rite? Such remote fancies were not to be gratified, however, for on enquiring from Francisca, several of the local topographers having failed to enlighten us, we learnt that they had been made for the use of charcoal burners, who had formerly plied an active industry in the Formentor peninsula.

The last few yards of the ascent were rough and stony and culminated in a great smooth slab of granite. Beyond this was the sky and below at a distance of some 800 feet the sea. It was an awe inspiring precipice and I began to feel that my weight might prove too much for the rock projection on which I was standing and that, if I stayed on it much longer we might both take off together and descend into the sea in rapid succession. An absurd but uneasy sensation, which it seemed unnecessary to prolong, so I retreated from the edge and we returned to the Villa.

******

The small boy, whose chief interest on our walks was in rabbit droppings, used often to enquire after our return to England when he could go back to "Brisas Bar", our regular rendezvous at Puerto Pollensa. I shared his nostalgia not only for the bar but for the Puerto. However, thirty five years had passed before we revisited Puerto Pollensa. By then both the bar and the Puerto, as we knew them, had disappeared. What we saw and from which we fled was a collection of concrete apartment blocks in various stages of construction. What we remembered is what I recorded at the time and have not altered.

Architecturally Puerto Pollensa is nothing; just a few low white houses with balconies resting on thin pillars, strung along the shore. Scenically it can scarcely compare with most of the other coastal towns of Majorca. What is it then that constitutes its special if discreet charm? I think it has something to do with the fact that Puerto - and it is a port, though a very small one - has no beach, *plage* or *playa*. The clear waters of Pollensa Bay lap the roadside and when you are sipping iced vermouth or eating a pistachio ice cream at the Bar of your choice, you may gaze across the calm water as the sun goes down, undistracted by the movement of beach wear across the foreground. The light and clarity of the sea seems to extend uninterrupted to the bright walls and interiors of the shops and neat hotels that line the front and even to the streets behind, where Puerto Pollensa reaches its limits and where we once caught a glimpse of Errol Flynn pausing on the pavement beneath a broad brimmed hat. It is reflected perhaps also in the manners of the barmen and shopkeepers, the mechanics at the garage and the lady who operates the petrol pump, each of whom appeared to us to be richly endowed with the Majorcan capacity to please.

Another attraction that the Puerto had for us was the ever hospitable house of Francisca and Fernando. Built on one floor, it enclosed on three sides a small garden that enchanted us with its fertility and artless beauty. It is the sort of garden that if I were to take Voltaire's advice literally, I should absolutely insist on cultivating. It is sheltered by the house from the winds that blow in from Pollensa Bay and Fernando is able to bask in the sun all the year round whenever his desultory gardening permits. Not that it needed to be very strenuous, for roses and grapes, lilies and peaches and other delights, including that beautiful but agonising looking plant aptly named Crown of Thorns, grew with the barest encouragement. Flowers and vegetables from the adjoining plot of land, which was also Fernando's property, were lavished upon us whenever we called and one evening we were entertained to supper, when Francisca effectively demonstrated to us that if she was economical in our house, no such consideration influenced her, when we were in hers. We sat down in the clean polished dining room at a table laid with glistening neatness, while Francisca bustled about, plying us with good things from her ultra modern kitchen. Fernando presided at the table with copious supplies of Binisalem wine, and later with a wide selection of liqueurs. When the feast was over we felt more than ever convinced that with its comfortable rooms and glamourous tiled bathroom, Francisca's house was an ideal home. All this and Francisca too! What a billet for an old soldier!

At the eastern end of Puerto Pollensa towards the mountainous confines of Formentor there are a number of villas whose gardens back onto an avenue of pines lining the shore. One of these villas, which had been built by a discerning Englishman* soon after the first world war, was inhabited by some American friends of ours and we were therefore privileged to taste the flavour of life as it may be lived by the shores of Pollensa Bay. The recipe is as follows:- Take a villa and fill it with good local furniture, engage two servants to do all the cooking, washing and housework, install chaises longues on the verandah which should give onto a small formal garden and beyond it the sea and hills, recline in the chaises longues, breathe the warm and fragrant air, eat and drink what is provided on the garden table and flavour with alcohol according to taste. There are variants of this recipe and additional ingredients for the more energetic. You may add for example, a small yacht which, when not at sea, will be moored to your own small stone jetty. You may also add a large and powerful motor car for use on the rare occasions when you feel the need of a change of food or scene.

*His name was Courtice. Was he perhaps connected with the famous Majorcan family of Cortés.

At the opposite end of the Puerto a more austere atmosphere prevails. Deprived of the shelter of the Formentor peninsula, the country is exposed to the full force of the Mediterranean, when it is behaving like a cruel sea and not like an expensive swimming bath. Here the sea shore is thickly covered with sea weed and we would often observe carts being loaded up with it or pass them fully laden on their way to the fields. George Sand thought this sea weed "was a very thin manure". The land is flat and except for one harassed grove of pines, treeless. There is also a small Albufera, a small "Little Sea" or marsh, which you pass before you reach the outer gardens of Alcudia.

Alcudia was dubbed the "most faithful" city by the Emperor Charles V for its refusal to take part in Majorca's peasants' revolt under Juan Crispin, and is generally considered the most "rancid" town in Majorca - "rancio" meaning rancid is the word used by the Majorcans to denote extreme age and stuffiness, to the point of sourness. Its reputation is supported by the vestiges of antiquity which are to be found in its immediate vicinity. The great gateway by which you enter the city - this is literally a courtesy title for a very small town - gives a suitably rancid first impression though it dates in fact only from the seventeenth century. The impression is confirmed by some rancid windows in the winding main street and by the other great gateway by which you leave the city.

But Alcudia's oldest vestige lies outside the gates just off the road towards Puerto Alcudia. It is a small Roman theatre believed to have belonged to the Roman settlement of Pollentia, which may have been situated where Alcudia now is. It has recently been excavated by American archaeologists and the historian and the tourist may now sit on one of its broken, worn and pock-marked tiers, hewn out of the solid golden rock, and reflect upon the decline and fall of the Romans in Majorca, while peasants toil more usefully in the fertile lands of La Puebla, which form a bucolic backcloth to the relics of the arena. Near the entrance of the theatre there is a man-made cave, whose use in Roman times can only be guessed at. It was subsequently used as a cow-shed, but that has now been stopped.

Our tourists' guide book upon which we largely depended for information about local things worth seeing, described in considerable detail an amphitheatre in the neighbourhood of Alcudia which, according to the author, was much larger than the theatre and in a remarkably fine state of preservation, quite incredibly fine in fact. From the photograph with which this description was reinforced, the author's enthusiasm certainly appeared to be justified. We were, therefore, a little disappointed on being directed at first to the smaller and obviously much less impressive ruin. When passing through Alcudia on subsequent occasions we made casual enquiries about the "gran anfiteatro" but received in reply protests of ignorance which we attributed in our intolerant British way to the usual inability of foreigners to give a straight answer to a straight question. One afternoon, determined to get to the bottom of the mystery of the "amphitheatre" we tackled an intelligent looking townsman, who after vainly trying, like the rest of them, to fob us off with the small theatre, said in the end that we must mean the bull ring and firmly directed us to it. We followed his directions, thinking scornful thoughts of the foolish citizen who did not know the antiquity of his own antiquities.

The "bull ring" was not difficult to find and we were admitted to it by an old man who unlocked for us a battered gate plastered with torn posters. We climbed up onto the topmost tier and saw that the ring was complete except for one place where a few stones were missing. The arena was grass grown and across it was stretched a volley ball net; "venerable monument" I fear we silently and tritely apostrophied as we were photographed against its hoary sides "to what tame purposes must you now be put" - "enough to make a gladiator turn in his grave" - "the grandeur that was Rome" - "How are the mighty", etc. etc. We left by the battered doorway feeling puzzled that such a well preserved Roman remain should not be better known, should not even be known apparently to the writers of other guide books.

The horrid truth was not revealed to me until some time later when I had read it in a brash waspish book on Majorca by an American, who for some reason enjoyed the patronage of the Fomento de Turisimo de Mallorca. This author informs his readers with evident relish and a wealth of documentary detail of the monstrous blunder committed by his rival in the field of Majorcan topography for tourists. After recalling the unfortunate man's prefatory and undeniably smug remarks about the inaccuracies of other writers, the Fomento's protegé positively revels in the idiocies resulting from a sad case of mistaken identity. For the bull ring is indeed a bull ring. There can be no doubt of it and to prove it our American scholar prints a letter from his dear friend the Secretary of the Ayuntamiento of Alcudia, stating that it was built in 1892 A.D.

Doubtless because of its impeccably rancid traditions, Alcudia was considered to be a fit place for the exile of Augustin Arguelles, one of the leading Spanish liberals, who suffered under the persecution of Ferdinand VII. A plaque used to record his stay in the town from 1815 to 1820, but I do not know if it is still there.

From the earliest days of their recorded history, the Balearic Islands and particularly Majorca have been used as a place of exile for heretics, liberals and others who have presumed to flout authority. Gibbon refers to an African bishop named Victor Tonnensiensis, who was banished to the Balearics, for having sided with the Western church against the Eastern in one of those obscure and superfluous theological controversies in the Primitive Church that used to excite the protagonists to frenzies of all uncharitableness. According to Tacitus, one Publius Sicilius "an informer in the Court of Claudius, banished under Nero by means of Seneca" (who was himself later banished to Corsica) was sent to the Balearics, "where he passed the remainder of his life in great pleasure and plenty." I can well believe it. What shocking heresy would one not commit if one had the certainty that banishment to Majorca would be the result!

\*\*\*\*\*\*

Being by the sea, for most people from Miami to Yalta, and often in spite of grimy pebbles and grey skies, is at the lowest estimation a minor pleasure of life and sometimes in certain circumstances it becomes a source of pure delight. Such circumstances are rare and we were fortunate to find them in one unblemished indentation in Pollensa Bay,\* whose exact location I may perhaps be forgiven for not disclosing, since to do so might possibly destroy one of those very qualities upon which its perfection depends. It may, however, assuredly be found by anyone who cares to look diligently for it.

\*Possibly in 1955 but not any longer.

22

That being by the sea should be delightful some elementary elemental conditions have to be fulfilled. The sun must shine brightly and strongly in a blue sky, the sea must be clear, neither too rough nor too calm and neither too hot, as it is in the tropics, nor too cold as it is almost everywhere else. Having secured this much, the seeker after perfection will require a stretch of shore, where the sun and the sea may be conveniently enjoyed. For this the necessary combination of qualities is seldom found since they tend to be mutually destructive. The shore must be easy of access, for the pleasures of the sea are not enhanced by a long and tiring approach, that becomes an even longer and more tiring retreat at the end of the day. Yet the chosen spot should be unfrequented and exclusive since the pleasure of being by the sea may be savoured to the full only in the privacy of solitude or select company and undisturbed by the presence or proximity of strangers. There must be sand to walk on or play with and rocks for many purposes, for shade and shelter, for lying on and under, for tables and chairs and diving boards. There should be little pools where shrimps abound and places where sea shells are found - shells of all colours: pink and purple, violet and green and rusty red, speckled and dappled, striped and mottled; shells of many shapes and sizes, some whorled like tiny cornucopia, some spiked like Siamese helmets, fans and bosses, cones and corkscrews, corrugated and dentellated, polished and barnacled, shells that form a moving patchwork irridescent at the water's edge. There should be sheltered waters in which you may lie when a breeze ruffles the sparkling sea, upon whose buoyant surface you may swim at ease without fear of treacherous current or voracious fish. And in order that you may not be oppressed by too great a feeling of isolation, there should be occasional alarums, as when a car is heard on the road above, or when a figure is suddenly observed on the rocks at the other side of the cove, clambering over them in search perhaps of mussels.

A place, having all these attractions we found, as I have said, on the shores of Pollensa Bay, and we used to go there as often as we could. We were evidently not alone however in our appreciation of it, though we never saw any of our fellow connoisseurs. Their houses and villas, the first of which had been built in 1873, were situated not far from our idyllic strand, but had not yet been opened up for the summer months. So if anyone should read this and hope to find what we found, he should go in the month of May.*

******

On the main road from Alcudia to Palma and not far from the town of Buger are some notices, urging one to visit the caves of Campanet. These, according to the guide book, have recently been discovered and are lit throughout by electricity. If you read further in the guide book, you will soon realise, if you did not know it already, that caves are a Majorcan speciality, even a national industry. The most famous are those of Arta, Hams and Drachs, generally accounted to be among the many natural wonders of the world. These you may visit and indeed can scarely avoid feeling morally bound to visit, so strongly are their attractions presented. You will be borne there relentlessly, in enormous motor coaches and before you know where you are, you will be gliding over the glittering bakelite black waters of underground lakes, to the

---

*It would now (1995) be a hopeless quest.

strains of Tchaikovsky and Wagner, you will be dazzled by floodlit stalactites and regaled with subterranean exhibitions of Majorcan folk-dancing.

Less dramatised and less frequented grottoes also have their charms, such as the Caves of Hercules near Cape Spartel, in Morocco, where mill stones are still chipped laboriously from the rock, and where the atmosphere is flavoured with generations of human excrement and where no tourist, perhaps for that reason, goes. The Caves of Artá were once as much neglected, though travellers were beginning to visit them already at the beginning of the nineteenth century. One of the earliest and most distinguished tourists to explore them was the great Spanish liberal statesman, Antillon, when he was the Spanish Central Junta's representative in Majorca. His account of the visit, which appeared in Blanco White's short-lived periodical, "Variedades", published in London, must be the first description of the caves in the English language. Antillon relates how he, like many others of less fame before and since, carved his name somewhere on the walls of the cavern, "Antillon, Montis, Victoria, 25 Setiembre 1811".

But the heroic days are gone now, when an enterprising Englishman could carry off mule loads of stalagmites* and when sporting English ladies, possibly with Raymond Lull's exploit in mind could ride horseback up the cavern's precipitous entrance.

There was in Majorca at least one cave which had not been popularised when we were there. Just beyond the east gate of Alcudia there was a discreet round blue notice board with white lettering and a white arrow, designed apparently to indicate the way to the Cave of San Martin. One rare afternoon when the weather was not quite good enough for the sands, we decided to see what the arrow led to. It seemed to lead at first metaphorically as well as literally, into the blue and we were soon lost among some barren fields on the edge of the Albufera. The rough track along which we were walking was bordered by the relics of abandoned enterprise. On one side there was a magnificent stone aqueduct, constructed ninety years ago by the English Company, about which more will be said later, and on the other side was the cutting for the extension of the Majorcan railway from La Puebla to Puerto Pollensa, a project never completed, owing to the outbreak of the Civil War.

We wandered uncertainly along the weed grown path between these two fruitless channels and eventually came across a countryman doing something backbreaking in a field. We were close to the Cave, he said, and pointing to some barbed wire upon a rising piece of ground, he resumed his stony toil. The barbed wire was quite shiny and had evidently recently been put up. It surrounded a large hole or crater in the field, into which a flight of stone steps descended. Entrance to these steps was given by a strong iron gate which however was securely padlocked. Since there appeared to be no-one to open the gate, I climbed over the wire, but only after it had extracted from me a small toll in blood. Having surmounted this obstacle I was on the point of descending into the depths, when the guardian of the cave arrived. He was not in the least put out by my forced entry into his domain, and after admitting the rest of the party, smilingly ushered us down the stairs into the hole in the earth.

*This piece of freebooting may perhaps have been redeemed by the offer of a later compatriot to pay 27,000 duros for the largest stalagmite in the cave that his predecessor had evidently been unable to remove!

At the foot of the steps, whose stone was dark green with the damp of centuries, we found ourselves in a kind of crude natural rotunda, in the centre of which was a well. This, our guide informed us, had been formerly used by the workmen employed by the English Company, when draining the Albufera. Some other pieces of stonework were of an ecclesiastical nature, notably an altar surmounted by a marble bas-relief depicting St George of Catalonia and Majorca, as well as of England, transfixing his dragon. This altar was set in a stone apse and in another niche, which had been fashioned into a small side chapel, were the relics of another altar. Heaps of dressed stone littered this niche and there were unmistakeable signs of restoration.

Our curiosity was aroused by this strange place and our gentle guide's vague allusions to its use by the early Christians fleeing from Roman persecution, made us all the more anxious to find out something about it. The Rector of Alcudia, a good and learned man, would be able to tell us all that was known, our guide assured us. Why did we not call upon him? He would be happy to receive us, our guide felt sure, and he for his part would be happy to introduce us. We took him at his word and after inspecting an ancient building near the cave, which, we were told, was of Roman construction, we drove off to interview the Rector.

I found him seated in a high-backed chair at his writing table in a room adorned with crucifixes and highly coloured religious prints. A small man, with a mild scholarly face behind black rimmed glasses, he welcomed me and invited me to sit down. I explained the object of my call and discovered at once that what interested us was something very near his heart. He explained that the shrine of San Martin, which within living memory had been totally neglected, had, in so far as the undergrowth with which it was choked allowed, been used merely as a shelter for cattle. To remedy this state of affairs and to restore the cult of San Martin had become one of the main preoccupations of his ministry.

The legend that the Cave had been used by the early Christians as a clandestine place of worship cannot, like most legends, be proved, and the fact that the Cave is dedicated to San Martin, favourite Saint of the Catalans, is seen as an indication that it may have been used originally by the first Catalan settlers, sometime before the eighth century. The cult of St Martin and also of St George was at all events firmly established soon after the Conquest (1229) and in 1507 there took place one of the many island miracles for which the Majorcans have so much enthusiasm. The countryside was suffering from a prolonged drought and in their distress the faithful turned to the Saint for succour. To present their plea, they went barefoot in procession to the Cave of San Martin and there they were rewarded for their pains. The Christ sweated blood and water, after which, the Rector told us, the rains came and the crops were saved.

As a result of this miracle, pilgrims flocked to the Cave in such numbers that a guest house was erected. A larger one was built in 1710 and this was probably the building which our guide had attributed to the Romans.

The retable which we had seen dates from 1632. There had been another retable in the other niche, which was dedicated to San Martin, but this had been mutilated and the fragments are now preserved in the Museo Luliano at Palma.

By the end of the eighteenth century the cult of St Martin had so much declined that his cave became a shelter for cattle and the Rector of Alcudia abolished the annual fiesta in 1827 and discontinued Sunday masses. Sixty years later, efforts were made by the Sociedad Arqueologica Luliana, to restore the two chapels but they failed, owing to the opposition of the local landlord, in spite of the fact that the Cave had been Church property since 1808. A further attempt was made by the Rector of Alcudia in 1908, but this likewise failed. The Rector was confident, however, that "God would send a virtuous man, who would complete the restoration of this ancient temple". His faith was well founded and his successor would appear to be this "virtuous man".

Don Antonio Beltran began the work of restoration in May, 1944, with the help of a number of enthusiastic young men, who volunteered their labour on Sundays. Money was also raised, with which to pay additional labour. Now, after eleven years (1955), the Cave must look much as it used to in the great days of the cult. One of the few guide books that mentions the Cave at all laments that this should be so, the author apparently preferring it as a refuse dump, to which it had finally been reduced. This is surely exaggerating the prejudice against restoration and though I may not entirely subscribe to the motives that inspire Don Antonio's efforts, I certainly hope they have by now been brought to a successful conclusion.

******

The circumstances in which we paid our first visit to Pollensa were scarcely auspicious. It was a dull, chilly day, our first in Majorca, and we were agitating about cots. Our landlord, who had done his best to convince us that we or the children ought to manage without them, had finally agreed to help us find some. At the Puerto he had failed to satisfy us with an antique crib he had unearthed in a cottage, so there was nothing for it but to extend our search to the local metropolis of Pollensa. We drove there up the long straight hill that leads from the Puerto through fields and orchards each enclosed by thick stone walls and passing under an avenue of plane trees, turned into a narrow street and entered the main square of the town.

There were not many people and no cars in the square at three o'clock in the afternoon and we had the whole of its well swept slightly uneven sanded surface in which to park. We drew up opposite a buff coloured building distinguishable from its neighbours only by a few discreet posters on its walls that identified it as the local cinema. Was it due to good taste or lack of money or sheer indifference that the somewhat plain features of the square had not been contrasted with a more brazen display of cinema advertisement? That good taste had once not been lacking in the municipality was evident from the stone fountain shaped like an Ali Baba jar and dated 1832, which stood close by lending with its graceful curves a touch of elegance to the otherwise prosaic contours of the square. They were further relieved by a raised flagstoned area, which formed a sort of inner square and the forecourt of the parish church. Here are steps and balustrades and a lamp standard or two, which strike quite a formal worldly almost frivolous note among buildings whose architecture is impressed with a work-a-day unself-consciousness. The note is muffled by a building that encloses one side of the forecourt. It had no front and was furnished with slabs. It looked like a fishmonger's and this it proved to be.

We were led by our reluctant landlord down narrow angular streets, sanded alleys - in Sussex they would be called "twittens" - whose bright diminutive shop windows displayed a coquettish neatness. We came to the cavernous entrance of a patio and were ushered upstairs to a room full of creaking polished wood. There we were invited to sit down and discuss the price of cots with the master carpenter and his family. We eventually decided on one painted a delicate blue. It was light too and very low, which was just as well for it soon collapsed under the weight of its occupant.

The best way to approach Pollensa is not, as we did at first, from the main Palma road, but from the road to Lluch and over the bridge that spans the torrent or, as it is for most of the year, the dried-up water course of San Jordi. On the left some hundred yards downstream is the small bridge said to date from Roman times and which is still in use, its stone roadway deeply rutted by centuries of cart and perhaps of chariot wheels. On the right is the beautiful hill at whose feet the town nestles. Its green terraces recalled to me a landscape of the Holy Land in a print of an Italian Renaissance picture vaguely remembered from childhood.

At the top of this hill is the celebrated Calvary of Pollensa, which is approached by a broad flight of three hundred and sixty five steps - one for each day of the year - flanked by cypress trees standing impassive and indifferent, like superhuman sentinels. One day we made our pilgrimage to the Calvary, the chapel of which was in the process of being redecorated. Adjoining it were the ruins of a lavatory whose floor was littered with fallen cherubs, their gilt rotundities having evidently been sacrificed to a more austere taste in ecclesiastical interior decoration. We tried to buy one of them but the negotiations got stuck somewhere and the cherubs may still be sprawling in their uncomfortable lavatory.

The simple chapel which houses the crucifix and two large and sombre Grecoesque pictures, does not command the touristic pilgrim's attention for long. He will soon wander away to the mirador and contemplate the famous view, which inspired some enthusiastic sentences in the severe Unamuno's "Andanzas y Visiones Españolas". He called it "una hostia de comunion con la naturaleza". Immediately below are the russet corrugations of Pollensa's tiled roofs and beyond and around them the fertile plain with its almond and fig trees and its crops of broad beans and oats. Behind and to the left are the rough and barren mountains, the highest crowned by the ruined castle known as El Castillo del Rey. Bounding the plain in front of us, are the lofty confines of our enchanted valley of Formentor and to the right are the waters, rather grey on this particular morning, of Pollensa Bay. Further still to the right and screening Alcudia's larger bay, is the precipitous hill on whose summit rests the nunnery of Nuestra Señora del Puig, celebrated in the local annals, for the escape of its breathless and corpulent inmates from sixteenth century Moorish raiders.

Pollensa is rich in religious institutions and buildings - even for a Majorcan town. There are three churches, of which the most notable is the former Jesuit church of Montesion. Dedicated to St Ignatius and built between the years 1697 and 1738, this large church is a typical if slightly meretricious example of Jesuit ecclesiastical architecture. The austerity of its massive west front is relieved only by the architrave of the baroque doorway. The interior almost gives the effect of a marble hall, almost, because the marble of the pilasters does not shine and on closer inspection we find that it has been somewhat crudely simulated by distemper.

The church was used by the Jesuits for only thirty years after its completion and after a few more years, during which the adjoining monastery was occupied

rather unwillingly by Capuchins from Palma, it ceased to be used as a place of worship and became a ballroom. Gradually it fell into disrepair and seems finally to have been abandoned even as a place for parties, for which it can scarcely have been ideally suited. A scandalised F.R.G.S. who visited it in 1886 reported that an altar was still there and above it a copy of a Murillo "very well painted by a young artist of Pollensa, of so much talent that he has gone to Rome to study his craft." Soon after this the church was restored and in 1891 reconsecrated through the efforts of the great Majorcan poet, Costa y Llobera.

The adjoining monastic buildings are now used partly as the offices of the municipality and partly as a boy's school, which is run by the Theatine fathers. It was one of the small boys from this school, who unlocked the church for us and later showed us over the classrooms. They gave an impression of uncomfortable shabbiness as most schools do and, although it was mid-morning on a week day they were quite empty. The schoolrooms certainly did not pulsate with youthful cerebrations nor did the football field, a walled enclosure about the size of a badminton court, resound with "follow ups" or ricocheting leather. Yet it must certainly have been term time. The only sign of life was in a small room at the end of a rickety passage to which we were admitted as a special favour by our small and eager guide. The room was little more than a cubby hole dimly lit by a small window, opaque with cobwebs. One wall was lined with cages filled with depressed canaries, contemplating, with drooping heads, the floors of their abodes, thick with droppings and unwanted food. The smell was indescribable and we hurriedly left this retreat of silent singing birds, the property, we were told, of the headmaster.

C.W. Wood, in his "Letters from Majorca", relates how he was told by the Archduke Luis Salvator of the manner in which canaries were first introduced into Majorca. He, the Archduke, had met one morning, wandering in his grounds, a stranger with whom he had got into conversation. The stranger explained that he had just lost a dear friend, who belonged to the island, and that in order to perpetuate his memory, he had brought with him to Majorca a number of canaries which he had set at liberty in the grounds of Miramar. "You have no canaries in Mallorca," he told the Archduke, "but why should they not live in your beautiful climate as well as elsewhere? At any rate, if they thrive, they will propagate, and their sweet song will be an everlasting chant and requiem to the memory of my dead friend. None shall know him; no other record of him shall appear." Perhaps the schoolmaster's canaries are the descendants of the unknown mourner's "little yellow songsters", their coronach now pathetically silenced.

Not far from the Montesion church is a small square in the middle of which is a stone fountain in the shape of an urn, surmounted by a cockerel. A "pollo", meaning a "chicken", is the crest of the town of Pollensa. It is a suitable crest, not only because the name Pollensa may have been derived from the word "pollo",* but because the town is largely populated with hens. You will see them in almost any courtyard of any house in any street, cage upon cage of them, busily laying the excellent eggs which you may buy at the rate of sixteen pesetas a dozen (in 1955!).

*The name of the Roman settlment of Pollentia is derived from *pollere* meaning to flourish.

Whenever other diversions allowed, we would drive into Pollensa to do our marketing, as most things were slightly cheaper there than at the Puerto. We bought wine from cool wine shops lined with barrels; we bought fish, prawns and squid from the fish market in the square, eggs from one of the houses of hens; potatoes, oranges, artichokes and lettuces from the vendors who heaped their wares on the raised flagged platform, where the market is held by the West door of the Church.

Whenever we visited Pollensa there invariably appeared to be something going on at the Pollensa Club, such as an art exhibition or once, no doubt the devoted work of some imaginative citizen, an exhibition of magazine covers. Clearly the Club had gone a long way since its inauguration in 1899 by the enthusiasts of cycling, a sport that had then recently been introduced into Majorca. Culture would now appear to be the dominant note in the Club's activities, and culture is a persistent, if not the dominant note in the life of Pollensa and its immediate neighbourhood. Artists and poets both foreign and of local stock abound and their works are for sale at Pollensa, at the Puerto and at Formentor. Rubén Darío wrote of the neighbourhood:

*Hay un aire propicio para todas las artes.*
*En Pollensa ha pintado Santiago Rusiñol*
*Cosas de flor, de luz y de seda de sol.*

The air is propitious for all the arts.
In Pollensa, Santiago Rusiñol has painted
Flowers and things of light, silk and sun.
*El Canto Errante*

So propitious is the air to artistic pursuits, that a nobleman, born and bred in Pollensa, determined that it should be of benefit to the artists of the world. "The last descendant of the family of Aloy, Don Pedro, planned the construction of a gigantic building at the Cala de San Vicente, as a free residence for the comfort of the intellectuals of the world, philosophers, printers, poets, men of letters, scientists, whom he proposed to invite to come and enjoy a period of tranquillity. The keys of each room were to be of gold. The building was to have an immense courtyard onto which all the windows would have looked. However, Don Pedro - Maecenas and altruist - died in Barcelona long before our war of liberation [the Civil War] - his death has remained a mystery - without it being possible to begin the construction of the projected palace."

This quotation is taken from the writings of Señor Miguel Bota Totxo, himself a poet, who must surely have done more than any man, to keep alive the cultural tradition of his native Pollensa. They told me how to find him when I asked at the bookshop at the Puerto and one day we called on him at the Alhambra Bar opposite the "Cockerel" fountain, appropriate situation for the resort of Pollensic literature. I found Don Miguel behind the bar. Gentle and sensitive, he received us kindly and gave me at once of his time and his knowledge as well as two of his books (on the *Calvario of Pollensa* and the *Cala de San Vicente*). He provides good evidence of the cultural properties of the air of Pollensa, which has reason to be grateful to its ardent and indefatigable publicist.

The Cala de San Vicente is a beach some four miles from Pollensa, where there is a break in the great cliff wall of the north west coast. We visited it one afternoon, but although we could not fail to be impressed by the immense rock sides of the Cavall Bernat, we did not share Don Miguel's enthusiasm for the Cala itself. The bare slopes leading down to the two small beaches are speckled with newly constructed villas, which, though they had destroyed the natural wildness of the place, had so far failed to civilise it. It is not easy to imagine what effect Don Pedro's palace would have had on the Cala, and one can only speculate whether its intellectual denizens would have hastened the process of civilisation.*

******

Picafort, half way round the shores of Alcudia Bay, is probably unique among Majorcan seaside places in that it caters exclusively for Majorcans and for that reason it is of particular interest. Situated at the end of a dusty road, which skirts the Bay, it seemed strangely remote when we drove out to it one very hot day in May. Its one wide sandy street, which merged at the far end into burning sand dunes was deserted, and the slightly gimcrack gaudily painted houses glared inhospitably in the sun. Beyond the sand dunes there were pools of stagnant water and near these a couple was sitting, their backs turned immovably towards us. Our first impression of Picafort was distinctly depressing.

We turned down a sandy alleyway between the houses and found ourselves on the "front" to which the entire population of Picafort had evidently repaired, so that there was little room left on the narrow strip of sand for anyone else. The "front" was still in an embryonic state and scarcely a suitable terrain for motor cars as we were soon to find out. We drove on to a deceptively firm piece of turf, but when the time came to move, the wheels refused to serve their purpose and, spinning furiously round, gouged holes in the sand until the back of the car was buried up to the axle. Meanwhile a number of onlookers had come forward to help and after strenuous exertions, we eventually extricated the car. Whereupon we retired to the local bar and fifteen of us had drinks at prices approximately ten times cheaper than at a bar in a tourist resort. After this experience we felt quite differently about Picafort.

Our party of helpers gradually dispersed from the bar and the family of the owner sat down to their mid-day meal. We followed their example and ate Francisca's cold *Granada* near one of the white obelisk shaped towers which line this part of Alcudia Bay and which are said to have something to do with submarine exercises. Some of our friends from the bar were near by having their food and, not to be outdone in hospitality, offered us pitchers of water from a neighbouring well, which they insisted was particularly sweet. I was a little doubtful of their recommendation, but having tried it, found they were not exaggerating. It was well worth offering to a stranger ignorant of its quality and on the strength of two economical and successful experiments in conviviality, we left Picafort, roasting in the sun and in a blaze of cordiality.

*The rock sides of the Cala have been covered with apartment blocks

*"Alcudia, a decent inn. It is the centre of some extensive works undertaken by an English Company with a view to drain and cultivate the marshes, which formerly produced only ague and sanguine hopes."*

O'Shea *Guide to Spain and Portugal* (1889)

Just beyond Alcudia and along the shores of the Bay there stretches a large expanse of marshland known as The Albufera. It is mentioned in most books on Majorca regretfully but not without a grudging affection. The Albufera is in fact the one blot on the otherwise fair landscape of the Majorcan lowlands. Where all else is industrious, productive and tame, the Albufera is wasteful and wayward, given to violence and apparently quite incorrigible. Miguel de Vargas, writing in 1787, described its waters as "pernicious" and the cause of a "very unhealthy climate in the surrounding country". Yet it can scarcely always have been so bad, for Dameto, writing more than a hundred years before de Vargas, does not mention its baneful effects. "Passing now along the coast of the city of Alcudia, the first thing that presents itself is a Pond of Water, our great Lake, to the South, which to this Day preserves its Arabic name of Albufera,* i.e. a little sea. There is in it plenty of very good fish; as also on its banks a great variety of birds, swans, ducks and other water fowl, which build their nests amongst the green flags and reeds, rendering this place very pleasant; it is 12,000 paces in compass."

Modern writers on Majorca, however, describe the Albufera in terms similar to de Vargas, but they also add vague references to the efforts of an English Company during the nineteenth century to drain it, efforts which were finally abandoned.

My curiosity was aroused by these hints of heroic if unsuccessful Victorian pioneering and, as the Albufera is not far from Formentor, I decided to devote some of my stay in Majorca to investigating it. I did not have much information upon which to base my researches. The books that I had read mentioned a family named La Trobe Bateman as having been the chief promoters of the Albufera scheme. According to one book the family achieved such eminence in the island that a Mrs La Trobe Bateman was known as the "Queen of Majorca". They were apparently as rich as they were eminent and they had residences at El Torreno, the smart suburb of Palma, and at La Puebla, the capital of the Albufera region. All the books agreed that the enterprise had come to an untimely end at about the end of the century, though for what reason was obscure. One writer attributed its collapse to "Mallorcan indifference to wealth that had to be won by too much exertion", but this statement, I suspected, owed more to prejudice than to knowledge.

People in the neighbourhood of Formentor whom I asked about the English company that had drained the Albufera, had never heard of it. I was beginning to be discouraged, when it occurred to me to ask Madalena who, I knew, was a native of La Puebla. She had heard vaguely of the company, she told me, and what is more, she could show me a bridge that was still called the "Puente Ingles". This was exciting news and it was decided at once that

*There is a larger and better known Albufera near Valencia, which Gustave Doré visited during the course of his Spanish travels.

we should make an expedition to La Puebla with Madalena and her little boy, whom Henry, in his novelist's way had arbitrarily christened, Gonzalez. Then with her relation's house as a base, we would undertake some serious enquiries in the town.

Accordingly, we set off one hot morning and were soon at the cross roads, where the dusty secondary road to La Puebla joins the main Palma-Alcudia highway. We slowed down and passed a group of tourists eating their sand-wiches by the roadside. We passed their two motor coaches and beyond them we passed, sprawled on the road, his blood-spattered twisted face staring at the sky, the body of a dead man, a motor cyclist, whose battered machine lay on its side a few yards off. We continued towards La Puebla, where we became at once the centre of interest. The whole town had already heard of the fatal accident and everybody wanted to know who the victim was. Questions were shouted at Madalena from every door and window as we proceeded slowly up the main street. "Who was it?" "Un forastero", a foreigner - meaning a Spaniard - she shouted back and no further interest was shown.

We arrived at the relation's house and after we had been introduced and made welcome, I explained the object of our visit to a stoutly built, strong-faced woman, who seemed to be the dominant personality among the rela-tions and who, I gathered, was Madalena's aunt. I could hardly have applied to a better person, for she knew very well the name of Bateman, which she pronounced Bartiman. She disappeared into the house and returned with a copy of the programme of the La Puebla Patronal Festival for 1946, which contained some notes on local history and local worthies, including an article on the Bateman family, "whose memory will be for ever linked with this town", and a photograph of Señor Luis [*sic*] La Trobe Bateman.

The aunt then spoke of a Viejecito, a little old man, whom Madalena had mentioned as being a likely source of information, and I was thereupon escorted to a neighbouring street and there introduced to him. He was waiting in the middle of the road with a slightly younger little old woman, apparently already aware of what I had come about. He told me he had worked for "Señor Bartiman", who was a good man, he said, but who had lost everything and had been obliged to surrender the Albufera to Señor Torrella. It was like a garden in the days of "Señor Bartiman" but now there was nothing but weeds. I asked him about Mrs B., the "Queen of Majorca". He knew about her too. She was called Beatriz and she was an "*artista*", he thought, whom "Señor Bartiman" had brought from Barcelona. The little old man's Spanish was very bad and even with the assistance of his little old wife, I found it difficult to understand what he had to say. I wanted him to accept a *copita* for his trouble, but in spite of his obvious poverty - he was dressed almost in rags - his little old wife declined vehemently on his behalf, and I left them still standing in the middle of the hot dusty street.

I returned to the house to find the whole party in the parlour seated at a round table on which glasses were set. Clearly we were not going to be allowed to proceed with the business of the day until the requirements of hospitality had been satisfied. I took the place appointed for me and the bottle was produced. It was a sweet liqueur called Palo, tasting not unlike Cointreau, which is manufactured from figs in the neighbouring town of Llubi. Perhaps not the Englishman's idea of the perfect "elevenses", but we sipped it gratefully and marvelled at the kindly generous manner towards strangers and foreigners of this good-natured people. After being shown the house with its spotlessly clean tiled floors and its elegantly carved furniture, we sallied forth once more into the bright sunlight.

Our first stop was at the local bookshop, where I hoped to discover something more about the Albufera and the English Company. I explained my business to the girl at the counter and was introduced to the owner of the shop, a black-haired man, who looked at me severely through thick spectacles. He was quite ready to help me, however, invited me into the room behind the shop and placed on the table all the volumes of the local literary review "Sa Marjal". This publication, which flourished during the early years of this century, was founded largely as a result of the efforts of the parish priest and is an admirable testimony to the liberal and on the whole enlightened character of the modern Majorcan priesthood. That so small a town should have had its own literary review (which I was told was to be revived) also provides further evidence of Majorcan interest in culture and the arts.

The bookseller assured me that there was a long article on the "Bartimans", in one of the twenty odd volumes and I began to look doggedly through them. As I turned over the pages I became aware that the bookseller and his wife and daughter had been joined by several citizens who, from their conversation, I judged must be pundits brimming with local lore. They were clearly anxious to help and soon each of them had taken a volume of "Sa Marjal" and was busily flipping over the pages. I left them gratefully to it, announcing that I was going to the Ayuntamiento and would return later to see the result of their researches.

The Ayuntamiento or Municipal Offices, forms one end of the main square which, by contrast with the hot dusty streets, is fresh and cool beneath its avenues of plane trees and is kept so by frequent douches of cold water on its pavements. The Secretary of the Ayuntamiento, into whose office I was shown, was obviously a very busy man, much busier than any of the other inmates of the building, whose principal occupation seemed to be to inflict upon him tiresome interruptions like myself. In spite of his preoccupation with the cares of office, he received me with great courtesy but explained, on hearing my business, that he was not deeply versed in local history. He was not a native of Pollensa nor even of Majorca, but like many of the Government officials in the island, a Spaniard. Still he did know about the "Bartimans", and he was able to show me a copy of the Royal Decree giving possession of the Albufera to John Frederick Bateman, which is apparently the only relevant document in the municipal archives. After I had received from him some suggestions about possible sources of further information and a promise of any help I might think he himself might be able to give, I took my leave and returned to the bookshop.

All was now quiet in the back parlour, the eager pundits having done their work and departed. The volumes of "Sa Marjal" had been returned to their shelves except one that lay open upon the table, displaying a photograph of an elderly and bewhiskered and very Victorian gentleman, John Frederick Bateman. The article on him, like everything else in "Sa Marjal", was in Mallorquin, which I could not read. So I made a note of the Volume and page, thanked the severe bookseller and left.

The article in the programme bequeathed to me by Madalena's aunt gave the address of the house and offices formerly occupied by the Batemans. Madalena led us there and we noticed on our way that one of the streets was called Calle Greene, a remarkable name, we thought, for a street in this small

Majorcan town. The Casa Inglesa, as it is known, is an unpretentious grey building, with a single iron balcony. It was shuttered, silent and deserted. The owner, we were informed, was in America and no one had lived in the house for some years. The days when it had been the focal point of the activities of the entire neighbourhood seemed remote indeed and we turned away from it to resume our pilgrimage.

We were now to explore the Albufera itself, with Madalena still acting as our guide, and if possible we were going to find the Puente Ingles. After nearly running down a doctor, who was gyrating dangerously on a motor bicycle in the middle of the road, we drove out of La Puebla and headed for the great marsh along a dusty track. As we advanced slowly, waiting for cattle to let us pass, Madalena dilated enthusiastically upon the paper factory we should be seeing shortly and for which she evidently felt some pride. We came to a bridge with bent cast iron railings and a roadway made of planks, which rumbled and creaked quite alarmingly as we crossed it. On the other side a peasant in a broad brimmed straw hat stopped us and, as we had been warned, levied on us a fee of ten pesetas for the privilege of using the road - if such it could now be called - which gave access to the paper factory, traversed the centre of the marsh and would lead us ultimately, we hoped, to the Puente Ingles.

It was with considerable misgiving that I turned the car into it, but having got so far, we could not very well turn back without losing rather too much face. I doubt if a car had ever been along that road before. It was in fact nothing more than a deeply rutted cart track, upon which there were also the marks of bicycle tyres. We lurched along it in low gear, bucking and bumping over the rough places, sinking and skidding into the deeper ruts, and brushing against the bushes and brambles that constantly threatened to block our further progress. I clung, grimly no doubt, to the steering wheel, feeling that if we stopped we should never get out of the marsh. Each side of the track there was a wide canal or dyke and beyond a waste of gigantic reeds. It was impossible to turn the car even if I had wished to; the only hope was that we would finally emerge at the other end onto a better road.

My mind was busy with anxious speculations over the possible fate of the car and ourselves, should the road prove impassable, when Madalena, with a shout of triumph, almost of exultation, announced that we were passing the paper factory on our right. I caught a fleeting glimpse of a chimney rearing its brick head among the reeds, but some particularly bad ruts made sight-seeing at that moment too hazardous for enjoyment and I am sure we did not pay the factory the attention Madalena felt it deserved. Soon afterwards we came to a slight upward slope in the track and at the top of it our hopes were rewarded, for ahead of us, spanning the canal, was a fine stone bridge of five arches - "el Puente Ingles". There it stood, solid and apparently untouched by its ninety years, amidst the waste of reed, amidst "the mist and hum" of the Albufera, a reminder of a great enterprise. Near by there were other reminders in the shape of bent and rusty sluice gates and, where the canal met the sea, the shattered ruins of two stone jetties. We paused a while over these interesting and melancholy vestiges and then hurried home for luncheon.

My friend the Secretary made good his offer of further help and in due course, in answer to my request, I received from him a Spanish translation of the article in "Sa Marjal". Though some of the statements contained in it I subsequently discovered were not accurate, I shall quote it in full, since it is revealing both of Majorcan character and their attitude towards the English:

Señor Bateman - Justice and gratitude ought to be denied to no one, whoever he may be; and for that reason, although an Englishman and a Protestant, it would be a grave fault not to say anything of Don Juan Federico Bateman and his grandiose work. A very long time ago, perhaps two thousand years ago, the Albufera, formerly called the "little sea" was united with the "great sea", which almost certainly came right up to the site of our town (La Puebla), as is clearly shown by the geological nature of the soil of our fields (marjales) formed by the sediment, robbed from the plain and the mountains by the torrents of Muro and San Miguel. This great lagoon, with an area of 5,000 acres, which in winter, was full of water and in summer became a number of large ponds, was the cause of such serious epidemics of malaria in the surrounding towns and principally in La Puebla, that even after the passage of half a century* it still has the reputation of being unhealthy, though the population enjoys robust health and the town, according to a recent statement by a doctor, has the lowest death rate in Spain.

Formerly, because there were very many woods and pine trees or for other reasons, it used to rain much more than it does now and therefore there were frequent inundations and overflowings of the torrents, whose waters remained imprisoned, as they did not flow into the sea, as they do now by the Grand Canal. Instead they formed a veritable "little sea" and at times, so to speak, a "large sea" when they flooded everything, not only the meadows of the Albufera, but also the immense lands of "Sa Marjal". The famous inundation known as "d'en Jelat", which took place on the 30th November 1852, and many others which caused very severe damage to the farms and also the many epidemics of fevers (tertians), which every year afflicted the neighbouring towns, led to serious efforts to find a remedy for such evils. At different times efforts had been made to canalise the waters to drain the Albufera, but the enthusiasm of the promoters was always dissipated in the face of indifference and neglect.

In the year 1853 the Director General of Public Works commissioned the distinguished engineer, Don Antonio Lopez, to study exhaustively, the question of the Albufera in order to resolve so pressing a problem. He did in fact study the matter and put forward a plan which earned the approval of the authorities and much praise from intelligent persons.

To put this plan into operation a Company of Majorcans was formed in 1854, the directors of which were the distinguished landowners of Muro, Don Claudio Marcel and Don Mateo Ferragut. They constructed the following canals: den Ferragut, de S'Viastre, den Molinas, den Conrado and den Palet which was only half completed.

In the month of March 1862 there came to La Puebla an English Company, which examined the ponds of the Albufera, the spring of Son San Juan and the soil of the meadows, of which a quantity was taken to London for chemical analysis. The director of this Company was Mister Juan Federico Bateman, who later became the sole owner of the Albufera. He was then fifty years old, of an amiable countenance and very kind (simpático) as can be seen from the photograph, which we have in our possession.

Very soon some English engineers arrived, the first of whom was Mister Guillermo Greene and later the well-known Mr Enric Waring, who lived for a long time among us and who died a little while ago at Palma. The operations of the colossal British enterprise did not begin until the 28th April, 1863, when the concession was officially granted to the illustrious gentleman Mister Juan Federico Bateman and Mister Guillermo Hope, very rich English lords. When the

* The article was written in July 1916.

enterprise was in the hands of these gentlemen, who came from England full of illusions and money it developed in an extraordinary way. Though it is true that the labourers had to work with water and mud, they were paid a daily wage of eight to twelve reales (8.3p - 12.5p) which at that time was a very high wage and for that reason, although the work was unhealthy, a large number of workers flocked to it; English, French, Ivizans, Mahoneses, and from almost all the towns of Mallorca: as far as from Manacor and Ses Salinas they came to work for "The Enterprise", so that at one point some fifteen hundred people were employed, each of whom was paid in gold coins every fortnight; when an amount totalling some twenty thousand duros was distributed (a duro then equalled approximately 20p).

Originally it was decided that the Works would have to be completed by the end of September 1867, but after that date they had to be continued due to the malarial fevers which occurred periodically with frightful intensity.

On the 6th February 1868 a year's postponement was granted in order to finish the gigantic works and on the 12th May 1870 a further seven months until the end of the year were granted. The English Enterprise did in fact finish the works by the end of the year, though the completion was not officially recognised until the following February.

Finally by Royal Decree on the 15th November 1871 the English Company was given the freehold of the land drained, amounting to 2,882 cuarteradas, which, together with what was subsequently bought from the Son San Marti estate and some other properties, amounted to a total, as we have said, of some 3,882 cuarteradas (a cuarterada is a Balearic measure equalling 7,103 square metres). Some time later the partners in the British company sold all their shares to Mister Juan Federico Bateman, who never ceased to carry out important improvements.

A large volume would not suffice to give an adequate idea of the fabulous manoeuvres that were executed in order to drain the famous "little sea". The works, which were carried out to drain the Albufera seemed to be not those of Romans as one is in the habit of saying, but of giants; and there is no doubt at all that there has never been in our island any undertaking that can remotely be compared with this colossal enterprise. Let us note a few facts and figures just to give some idea.

There were three very powerful hydraulic engines, one of which was able to pump eighty cubic metres of water a minute; then dykes and canals, some of which were very large, were dug; the colossal "Canal Grande", which was constructed to channel the waters of the two large torrents of San Miguel or La Puebla and of Muro was 60 metres wide and 2,500 metres long; roads were constructed to a length of more than 40 kilometres or eight leagues; a jetty (or mole) was constructed of large blocks of stone, each of which must have weighed more than a hundred quintals (nearly five tons); this mole extended some 300 metres into the sea and was used either to load hemp for England or to prevent the Grand Canal from being silted up during rough weather; two enormous iron bridges were built and many more of masonry, whose piers rest on piles made of pine logs: the Canal Riego was constructed which surrounds almost the whole of the Albufera and is 72 kilometres or more than 14 leagues long and according to some well-informed people, cost a duro a palmo [21 centimetres] or 400,000 duros, etc. etc.

For the greater convenience of the workers on the Enterprise, in addition to Sa Vileta near La Puebla and the houses near the sea, the English built in 1876 the colony of Gata Moix, consisting of 22 houses between the Albufera and the Albufereta, and as they were sincere Protestants they wished that the Majorcans should fulfil their duties as good Catholics. Therefore, although it did not come about during the lifetime of his father, who died at the beginning of 1889, his very nice son Mister Luis [sic] Latrobe Bateman, on the 27th December of the same year amid delicious gardens and pastures, erected a classical Church with very rich ornaments and very valuable plate all in the English style. By Royal Decree on the 16th June 1892, the peculiar name of the Colony was changed to that of Colony of San Luis.

In the house, inhabited by the Bateman family (La Puebla, Calle de la Plaza, number 1), there was a private chapel with an altar and crucifix where they used to hold frequent services. One of the sons of Don Juan Bateman (the son who was Rector of a London parish and very exemplary and charitable) about the year 1892 came to spend the whole winter at La Puebla and brought with him his daughter, a young girl of about eighteen, who was very devout. His other son, Don Luis [sic], who was much younger than the former and was then only 33 lived for some years among us and was so good that he earned the grace of being converted to Catholicism and as he belonged to the English aristocracy (together with his wife who was very handsome) he was reconciled in the year 1893 with the Catholic Church by the most wise and famous Cardinal Manning, who also was converted from Protestantism many years before to become the Apostle of England and who, as a wedding present, gave them a magnificent and de luxe English edition of his complete works in nine volumes, which when they returned from London, they showed us with great joy and with the innocence of the freshly baptised. During the time that these English lived among us, equally before as after their conversion, they always set a very good example. Our great benefactor, Don Juan Bateman resided normally in London, whence he directed his great enterprise through his own engineers, but from time to time he came to La Puebla. For the New Year celebrations of 1886 he came, among our countrymen, who fêted him prodigiously. In the large and spacious house of Pedro Antonio Serra, which was formerly the residence of the March family, a large reception was held in honour of the Englishman, who was regaled with speeches and verses ....

About the year 1886 Don Juan Bateman gave, as a small part of his vast possessions, the property of the Albufera and the adjacent lands to his son Luis [sic], who administered them on his own account until, considering that things were going badly for him and that such a rich property would ruin him, he handed it over to the noble gentleman of Palma, Don Joaquin de Torrella, who took possession of it on the 10th March 1896 and who has since then carried out some important works on the property.

The draining of the Albufera, which formerly was thought to be impossible, became a reality. Happy are we, who have found the work accomplished! But ... if we could see the hundreds and thousands and hundreds of thousands and even millions of dollars lavished on such a colossal and useful enterprise, we should be horrified. People who ought to know, have assured us that more than three and a half million duros were spent on the Albufera."

To this account the Secretary was able to add one or two more pieces of information he had gained from hearsay among his friends at La Puebla. According to them Don Luis Bateman had failed because, when he became a Roman Catholic, his kinsman, the Dean of Canterbury, refused to advance any further subsidies for the scheme. Also Don Luis had a beautiful carriage in which he visited the Albufera and instead of a horn or a modern klaxon he used a conch to warn pedestrians. When he went to Palma he went in a special train. As for his payment of the men's wages in gold coins, that "attracted attention".

The affection in which the people of La Puebla and the immediate neighbourhood still hold the name "Bartiman" was illustrated by an incident that took place some time after our exploratory visit to La Puebla and the Albufera. In the course of conversation with one of the workmen, who helped to dig us out of the sand at Picafort, I asked whether he knew anything about the

English company that had drained the Albufera. He had certainly heard of it and indeed his mother possessed a picture of "Señor Bartiman". I said I would like to see it and it was at once agreed that I should call on his mother the following evening. He promised to be there also if he could, but in any event he would warn her to expect a visitor. I called as arranged at his mother's house in one of the broad straight streets of La Puebla, and the portrait was brought into the front room for my inspection. It was a large photograph of a mild-looking man with smooth hair parted in the middle and a moustache drooping somewhat weakly at both ends - clearly identical with the picture of Luis Latrobe Bateman in the Patronal Programme. Why did she have this portrait, I asked. The husband, for so I took him to be, answered "Because he was a great man in the country", and went on to explain that after "Señor Bartiman" had left Majorca a certain enterprising photographer, who possessed a negative of a photograph of him, had made a large number of prints of various sizes, and these had been much sought after in the neighbourhood.

One afternoon, when the sun was not shining and the sea looked grey, we set out to find the colony of Gata Moix or San Luis or the Pueblo Nuevo, as it is now somewhat misleadingly called, and, after many enquiries and a call at a farm of terrifying squalor, we finally located it. To reach it, we drove up an earth road that winds steeply through pine trees, from a point on the main Palma road about three miles from Alcudia. At the top of the hill we came to a clearing, covered with weeds and heaps of stones in the midst of which stood a small house. From it emerged a scraggy dog barking hoarsely, followed by a shabbily dressed peasant. We shook hands and, after I had explained the reason for our visit, he showed me round all that was left of Pueblo Nuevo. It reminded me of photographs in the Illustrated London News of Flanders villages in 1918. Of several rows of houses all that remained were a few fireplaces, and the ragged stump of a chimney. One heap of masonry was once the fine "classical Church" of San Juan "in the English style", another was the school and another was the schoolmaster's house. A fig tree was growing in the reservoir, the roof of which had fallen in. Only the well and the house inhabited by my guide remained intact. He invited us in and we found ourselves in a large room, whose lofty ceiling was supported by beams of pitch pine. The doors were also made of the same wood. We penetrated to the garden behind the house and found a few chickens scratching among the weeds.

The man at Picafort had told me that the Pueblo Nuevo had been abandoned and had subsequently fallen into ruins because, having been built by heretics, it was feared by the people to be unwholesome. Similar reasons had been advanced by other informants, usually with expressions of contempt for the superstition that had given rise to such fears. The one remaining householder had a different story to tell. According to him, the landowner had evicted the tenants because he wished to demolish the village for the sake of the valuable timber "the English had brought from the North", that is the pitch pine they had used in the construction of the houses. Only one house had been preserved for the use of the tenant farming the surrounding land. Formerly it had been used as a kind of communal lodging house for workers who had no family or who were only temporarily employed on the estate and the large room in which we were standing had been their "refectory". As for the church, all that still remained of its past costly splendour was a figure of the Virgin, thought to have been made in England and now kept in the

Church of Puerto Alcudia.

On our way back to the car we lingered for a moment to look down over the smiling valley of Pollensa stretched below us, its fields and trees and houses serving to emphasise the desolation of our immediate surroundings. Beyond the clearing, the dark pine trees stirred uneasily in the wind; only the blood red flowers of a single pomegranate tree stood out starkly against this sombre background. It was possible to feel overcome with the melancholy of the place. Was it merely the sadness that must pervade any abandoned dwelling or any ruined enterprise, or was there really something about it that was unwholesome and which the local people had attributed to the English heretics or before them to the Moors? Had the site, with its healthy elevation, chosen by the English engineers for their model village with such care and foresight, been infected for ever by some horrid primaeval rite? Further speculations on these lines were interrupted by the arrival of the equally ragged wife of the last tenant of Pueblo Nuevo. We said good-bye to them and with relief, drove away.

This visit to the deserted village increased my determination to find out the full facts of the Albufera story and on our return to England I began to make further enquiries. These at first were not very successful. None of the name of La Trobe Bateman had been Dean of Canterbury, but there was, I discovered, a Canon La Trobe Bateman, who had been rector of Ascot. No amount of research would reveal any connexion between Cardinal Manning and the former owners of the Albufera, who it seemed must have quite disappeared without leaving any further traces. It was "Who's Who" that eventually led me by devious channels to the source from which I was able to learn as much of the story as probably can or need be learned.

John Frederick la Trobe Bateman was one of the great engineers of the nineteenth century, worthy to have figured among the "Lives" of Samuel Smiles, and whose name used to be commemorated with many of theirs above the windows of the City and Guilds College in Exhibition Road, now demolished. His father was an unsuccessful Yorkshire cloth manufacturer, but also a mechanical genius, who invented a harp with keys, which he called the Clavi Lyre. His mother was the daughter of a distinguished and pious Huguenot Moravian Minister, named Benjamin la Trobe. John Frederick inherited his father's mechanical talents and his mother's strong and lofty character, and the resulting combination produced a formidable example of Victorian eminence.

Apprenticed at an early age to a firm of Civil Engineers, at twenty-three Bateman had set up in business on his own account. It was not long before his outstanding abilities began to be recognised and at the still youthful age of twenty-five he was entrusted with some considerable drainage operations on the River Bann in Ireland. This was the first of many important undertakings chiefly in the sphere of hydraulic engineering, the most notable of which were the vast schemes for supplying water to the cities of Glasgow and Manchester. But Bateman's energies were not confined to the British Isles and his work took him as far afield as Ceylon, the Argentine, Mexico, Nova Scotia, Turkey, Italy, Malta, Spain and Majorca.

A man of wide vision as well of immense erudition, Bateman foresaw the tremendous increase in the size of many English cities, and the revolutionary steps that would have to be taken if adedquate suppliesof pure water were to be assured. In 1865 he turned his attention to the problem of London's water supply and after undertaking, at his own expense, a survey costing £4,000, presented to Parliament a scheme for supplying London with water from the watershed of the River Severn. The scheme was calculated to cost £11,400,023 and to supply the capital with two hundred and thirty million gallons of water a day. A Royal Commission under the Chairmanship of the Duke of Richmond, examined the project "but decided that for the present at least, the metropolis did not require so expensive a measure". Time has shown, however, that Bateman had not underestimated the future needs of the capital and today the Metropolitan Water Board supplies consumers with a daily average of nearly three hundred and twenty-two million gallons (this was the figure in 1955).

The great engineer evidently inherited some of his father's inventive genius, for in 1869 we find him publishing jointly with a Mr Revy what must be one of the earliest schemes for a Channel Tunnel, "a cast iron tube for carrying a railway across the Channel between the coasts of England and France".

In the same year he was sent out as the representative of the Royal Society on the invitation of the Khedive of Egypt, to attend the opening of the Suez Canal. In his report to the President of the Royal Society we have another example of that prescience, which so much distinguished him. He wrote, "The canal must be regarded as a great work, more from its relation to the national and commercial interests of the world than from its engineering features. In this light it is impossible to overestimate its importance. It will effect a total revolution in the mode of conducting the great traffic between the East and the West, the beneficial effects of which, I believe, it is difficult to realise." He concluded, too optimistically it turned out, "A channel of water communication has been opened between the East and the West which will never again be closed, so long as mercantile property lasts or civilization exists."

Bateman seems to have been happily conscious of his own virtues and proud of his success. In a letter to his dear children that he caused to be printed, we find him calmly reflecting upon "a family [his own] which had given up all worldly distinction for the sake of religion and conscientious duty, and amongst whose members not one could be pointed to as unworthy of the name or race." He refers complacently to "the profession in which I have been so successful", and attributes this success to the "application of natural talent and attention". His obituarists were later to find these revelations useful and taking their subject at his word, quoted him extensively, but without acknowledgement.

When confronted with such enormous self-satisfaction one can only wonder how the Batemans of the Victorian era were endured. The answer seems to be that, not only was a candid and just appreciation of one's merits preferred to modesty whether false or real, but that a certain humourless and insensitive stuffiness was at a premium in the circles in which they moved. How otherwise could an obituarist record, as if it were a matter of solemn moment, the fact that during Mr Bateman's Presidency of the Institution of Civil Engineers, "the Conversazione held on 4th June at the Indian Museum, South Kensington will be memorable, not only because it was in honour of the fiftieth anniversary of the incorporation of the Society by Royal Charter, but also on account of its being the first occasion on which ladies were not invited to the soiree; or more strictly speaking, it was a return to the old custom of the invitations being confined to gentlemen."

Yet with all his self-satisfaction, the great engineer had the sort of proud humility that refuses, as he did, the offer of a baronetcy, and a thoughtfulness for others that made him beloved by his servants. He was a good man according to his lights, and these could scarcely fail to be focussed in one direction, since he can have had little time for introspection or that agonising examination of the conscience to which many of his more leisured contemporaries and perhaps most of his grandchildren and their contemporaries were and are prone. This goodness found expression in the disinterested devotion to human well-being which was certainly as strong a motive as commercial profit in all his activities and in none more strongly than in the Majorcan enterprise.

I have not been able to discover precisely how or why Bateman came to hear of the Albufera and its possibilities of development, at a time when Majorca was so very little known to English people. He had, however, been engaged in 1862 in irrigation works in the valleys of the Henares and the Esla near Madrid and may have heard about the Albufera at that time. It is also possible that he may have read one of the very few English books in which an account of Majorca was to be found, Carr's "Travels in Spain and the Balearic Islands". If he had read this book, we may be quite sure he took note of the author's reference to the Albufera, which was to the effect that during his stay at Alcudia, "we were not sensible of any inconvenience from the lake, which might be easily and profitably drained".

In 1863 the marsh was purchased by the Majorcan Land Company of London, of which the principal directors were John Frederick Bateman and Colonel William Hope, the latter being also one of the directors of the Iberian Irrigation Company, with which Bateman had been associated. The work of reclamation, which was begun in 1864, was finished for the most part in 1871 and in 1877 "the well-known" Henry Waring, the engineer who "lived for a long time among us", was able to report in a paper read before the Institution of Civil Engineers a "remarkable improvement effected by drainage in the sanitary condition of the adjoining district, the population of which is rapidly increasing".

The total area of land reclaimed was 5,100 acres, and the main water course the "Grand Canal", along whose banks we had driven, was 164 feet wide and nearly ten feet deep. The canal's outlet to the sea was protected and preserved by two jetties of rockwork carried into deep water. Springs on the borders of the Albufera were diverted into embanked canals and their waters discharged into the main watercourse near the sea, through automatic flap gates. In addition nearly thirty miles of roads were constructed in the Albufera.

Although all these expensive works had resulted in an improvement in the sanitary conditions of the neighbourhood, it is evident that doubts were already being felt whether there would be adequate return for the huge capital outlay involved. As early as 1876 Consul Bidwell, who had paid a visit to the Albufera, in which he and his family were nearly drowned, was writing somewhat gloomily of the English Company which "a few years ago carried out at great expense, extensive works in draining land known as the Albufera near Alcudia, but these works are at present in abeyance."

In his paper Waring explained the difficulties with which the Company was faced. A sufficient return on their capital outlay could only be achieved if the land produced crops more valuable than oats. But the Majorcan tenants could not be persuaded to sow anything else and in view of the failure of an experimental crop of cotton, they are scarcely to be blamed. Later experiments by the Company with hemp and beans were more successful however, and as a result, some of the tenants were induced to go in for their cultivation.

Another and more serious difficulty was the shortage of labour. The newly drained land, being unsuitable for mechanical cultivation, the Company was obliged to depend on local labour, local farming methods and what was worse, the local system of land tenure. In the fertile island of Majorca, where almost everyone has a piece of land or at least a share in a piece of land, casual labour or tenants were and are, extremely scarce. There was much more land in the Albufera than could be effectively cultivated by the inhabitants of La Puebla and Alcudia, and it was with a view to attracting tenants from further afield and particularly from Pollensa, that the Company decided to build two new villages. One of these was the Pueblo Nuevo of Gata Moix.

Meanwhile the area under cultivation grew less and less, while the reeds whose growth had been encouraged by the draining, threatened to overwhelm everything. By 1877 only 857 acres out of the total area were being cultivated by four hundred and eighty three tenants.It was estimated that if the whole of the Albufera was to be cultivated, no less than twelve thousand tenants would be needed. No wonder that Mr Waring allowed a note of depression to creep into his paper.

He had one suggestion how the swamp might still be made to pay and justify the immense amount of capital expended on its drainage. It was that the reeds, whose growth had been so alarmingly fostered, might, if found suitable, be used for the manufacture of paper. He had had some experiments made, but at the time of writing was unable to say whether the reeds could be utilised. Evidently they proved to be suitable, for soon afterwards the Company established the factory, in which Madalena - and I can now see rightly - showed so much interest. It was the only thing that, financially speaking, saved the enterprise from being a total failure.

The Albufera is next heard of in a book written by a sententious and tiresomely jocose F.R.G.S. named C.W. Wood, who visited Majorca in 1888 and stayed with the Batemans both at Palma and La Puebla. Wood was dazzled by the beauty and charm of Mrs Lee Bateman who, he says, was known as the "Queen of Majorca". He was also as much impressed by the firm but patriarchial manner in which Lee - not Luis, as recorded locally - treated his tenants as by his generous hospitality and the splendour of his manner of living.

But the estate was in no condition to sustain such extravagance and financial stringency was already beginning to be felt, for soon after Wood's visit, the house had to be given up. The following year the "devout young girl", Rowena Mildred la Trobe Bateman, whose diary of her visit to Majorca has been preserved and made available to the author of this book, recorded how "we passed Uncle Lee's old house at Terreno, most beautifully situated in a lovely garden with a magnificent Panorama of Palma and surrounding country, washed by the waves of the blue Mediterranean".

Though she does mention "letters which made Uncle Lee rather uncomfortable, so he decided to leave us beauties and toddle to the North" (i.e. England), the maidenly diarist was evidently blissfully unconscious of the ruin which was by then threatening to overtake her uncle. Her diary reveals an entrancing, unsophisticated, high-spirited, slightly giddy, religious girl of eighteen, enjoying every minute of her six months' stay in Majorca. Usually in the company of her aunt, she is busy driving through the "splendidly cultivated"

Albufera or to Alcudia "whose walls belong to Uncle Lee" or to the "lovely little village" of Gata Moix; dousing the long-suffering but devoted servants with water; paddling with her skirts drawn daringly "above our knees" (was it not soon to be the Naughty Nineties?); staying at Palma with Consul Mark; admiring the vast proportions of the Cathedral; being welcomed by the genial Archduke Luis Salvator who "talked so fast and so much that we could none of us get a word in edgeways"; and riding on muleback from Soller to the summit of the Puig Major and then to the Monastery of Lluch.

She was also engaged in a discreet flirtation with "dearest Richard [dearest is crossed out in the manuscript], who is ever in my thoughts, and pays me constant visits, and is never tired of giving me proofs of his devotion." What sort of proofs, one cannot help wondering? He comes to luncheon and to tea and whenever he does there are coy exclamation marks and dashes and fluttering aposiopeses. Clearly the spell of the Greater Aphrodisiad is upon her. They go for lovely walks together, "rendered more delightful by the companionship of dear Richard", along the road to Buger, a name which we, sixty five years later, found difficult to take seriously.

Much of the diary is devoted to the church of San Luis, which was nearing completion. She describes how she and her aunt unpacked the altar furniture, plate and vestments sent out from England. She also gives a very full account of the Consecration ceremony to which she had looked forward with much excitement and to which weeks of preparation had been devoted. When the great day came at last, it started badly, for the special train, which Uncle Lee had arranged for the transport of distinguished guests from Palma, broke down, so that Mildred and her aunt were left waiting in the church, tormented, no doubt, by that particularly hopeless brand of suspense that overtakes best men in church, when either the bride or bridegroom are late. The dignitaries finally did arrive and the Consecration duly took place. It must, one feels, have been a somewhat tedious occasion, in spite of the fine weather, involving as it did, separate petitions for the blessing of the building by every saint in the Church calendar - 365 of them. The sub-Dean of Palma gave an eloquent address, much of which was dutifully recorded by the diarist. He paid tribute to the generous donors of the Church, which he prophesied would for many generations to come be a standing memorial to them as well as an unceasing benefit not only to hundreds but to thousands. Before he closed his address he called down a special blessing on "Uncle Lee and Aunt B." Alas the good sub-Dean's prophesy was not to be realised and his blessing not apparently to be effective.

After the Consecration ceremony the company drove to Alcudia where a feast had been prepared at the Batemans' summer house near the Albufera, called "La Roca". The guests entered under a triumphal arch of myrtle and found themselves in a room decorated "with all the English and Spanish Arms". Quantities of champagne were drunk and when,owing to the lateness caused by the breakdown of the train, candles were unexpectedly needed, Uncle Lee brilliantly solved the problem of candlesticks, enthusiastically records his admiring niece, by having the empty champagne bottles "recorked with tallow candles".

Empty champagne bottles might symbolise adequately the end of the story, for charming, feckless, dilettante Uncle Lee was rapidly getting through his share of the family fortune, inherited from his eminently stable papa. Occupied with his camera and his banjo, travelling in first class coupés across

Europe and by special train in Majorca, driving his elegant horses and blowing his eccentric conch, now playing practical jokes and now closeted upon his knees in his oratory, the unfortunate Lee had neither the time, the application nor the interest required to save the Albufera enterprise and himself with it from ruin. Whether or not his elder brother, later to become Rector of Ascot and a Canon of Oxford, who was then building churches at Norwood, refused to put any more money into the enterprise, is not known, but it would scarcely be surprising if the letter which made Uncle Lee so uncomfortable contained an intimation of some such intention. The Canon could hardly be blamed. To one, who was dedicating his fortune to the greater glory of Anglo-Catholicism, moneys which were apparently being lavished on an expensive Roman Catholic church admittedly in English style, for the use of workers on an unproductive marsh might well have seemed to be going literally down the drain. It is likely that the good man's fears were confirmed when his daughter returned to her family at the beginning of June 1890 after the most "SCRUMPTIOUS" holiday she had probably ever had in her whole life.

The end of that holiday was the beginning of the end of everything else. Uncle Lee gave up the Albufera and then, in spite of his reconciliation with the Roman Catholic Church, he gave up Aunt B. This was more than the family could stand - had they not already subscribed £70,000 towards his other extravagances - and he was sent off to America, whence after remarriage and a long exile he returned to his native land to die. Aunt B. did rather better and became Queen of another kingdom, when she married a Coal King, Sir Stephenson Kent, whose name used to be seen on almost any goods train in any part of England.

Of the other persons in the Albufera story, John Frederick Bateman had already died at Moor Park,* full of years and eminence, a few months before Mildred had left for Majorca. His original partner in the Majorca Land Company, William Hope, went on to gain distinction as an expert on sewage disposal, a field in which he collaborated with a fellow Scotch engineer, the Hon. William Napier. He also addressed a Royal Commission on the subject of "Warlike Stores" and towards the end of his life seems to have become involved in some litigation, as a result of which he published an "Appeal to the fourth estate with regard to Colonel Hope's Scotch title to certain Scotch property". Whether his appeal resulted in justice being done, I have not ascertained.

Of the engineers, Waring died, as we have seen, at Palma in 1913, but what happened to William Greene I have not discovered. Neither have I been able to identify "dearest Richard", but she to whom he had shown so much devotion died, it is sad to relate, unmarried.

*Moor Park, which is chiefly famous for its associations with Sir William Temple and Jonathan Swift, became a theological college of which the Principal was, by a strange coincidence, a grandson of John Frederick Bateman.

# CHAPTER IV
## SOME PLACES

*Un temps viendra sans doubt où les amateurs délicats, et jusqu'aux jolies femmes, pourront aller à Palma sans plus de fatigues et de déplaisir qu'à Genève.*

G. Sand

One fine day we went to Valldemosa, famous for the uncomfortable shelter it gave to George Sand and Chopin. We started early in the morning when the air was still keen and when the country carts crowded the main road to Palma on their way to field or market. At Santa Maria we took a turning to the right and drove along a narrow stony road, that led through olive groves and orchards of almond trees, a merry hill-strewn countryside. We passed through Buñola, toylike in its amazing neatness, with its absurd little railway station that looked as if it had been made by some continental Hornby. Soon afterwards we joined the Palma/Soller road which, in sixty hairpin bends, crosses over the pass that gives access through the mountains to the valley of Soller. The road was constructed with considerable difficulty by French engineers in 1850, after a great deal of their preparatory work had been destroyed by one of those tremendous storms, such as George Sand once experienced, which from time to time afflict the neighbourhood.

It was while crossing this pass that I smelt for the first time in my life the scent of lemon blossom. Then I knew or thought I knew what the poet had in his mind's nostril when he wrote:

*Kennst du das land, wo die zitronen blühn?*\*

For me that land will now always be Majorca.

As we zig-zagged towards Soller, roses nodded and becked from neat little gardens, their bright colours entwining the mountain side with a living garland. Here a vine's yellow-green bower cast a pale translucent shade and there a crystal streamlet caressed the moss covered stones of a terrace bastion. The dionysiac contortions of ancient olives were emphasised by contrast with the straight limbed trees of more northern fruits and, as we descended into the deep valley of Soller, the scene became one of lush fertility.

It was May 9th, a gala commemorative day for this town, so much blessed by nature, and the streets were crowded and en fete. There were booths and stalls and barrows laden with brightly coloured goods and there was all the machinery of a fair. Everything was drenched in sunlight and Soller, snug and, dare I say, a trifle smug in her fertile valley seemed to exude a knowing prosperity. Could it be that this festivity, which celebrates the repulse by the townsmen of a sixteenth century Moorish foray, had become tainted with "Turismo"? Was it all being self-consciously "laid on" for the benefit of the visitor? Had the gloomy forebodings of English Victorian travellers been realised and the sweet simplicity and native charm of Soller been spoilt by their myriad successors in search of what their grandfathers had loved and helped

---

\*I subsequently read that this poem had inspired J.B. Laurens with his desire to visit Majorca.

46

to lose? For Soller is a stronghold of the English, and pretty though she assuredly is, she does seem to behave like an English tea shop abroad, which also has its charms.

From Soller we drove down a magnificent tunnel of plane trees to Puerto Soller, which we found bulging with tourists. There were also some small warships, believed to be American, tied to the quay in the small mountain-encompassed harbour. Clearly there were already quite enough people in Puerto Soller, so we soon left it. We thought better of Soller and its Puerto when we stayed there twice thirty five years later, the second time in a country house high above the town. Bessie D. Beckett gave an account in her memories of Mallorca (1947) of her stay at Soller in a rented cottage. She wrote the book after her soldier husband had asked for one "free from war and free from sex".

We returned through the green tunnel and, passing a cripple minding a goat, took the road for Deyá, Valldemosa and Miramar, the Grande Corniche of Majorca. The country which this road traverses is chiefly associated with that amiable Hapsburg, the Archduke Luis Salvator, who came to Majorca in 1867 to seek solace after the death of his wife. He lived for many years at the house he built for himself, which he without originality but accurately named Miramar. During his long residence he devoted himself to the embellishment of his property, which gradually increased as he bought further stretches of the coast, in order to preserve its scenic beauties and particularly the trees from the indifference of the local inhabitants. Majorca owes much to this agreeable prince, including a massively Teutonic study of every aspect of the island's life and lore.

The road winds in and out of the folds of the precipitous and wooded coastline high above the sea. There was very little traffic on it that morning and nothing except our own car to disturb the serenity of the air. If the belief that romantic surroundings can bring solace to a grief-stricken spirit is not a mere pathetic illusion, then the Archduke could hardly have chosen a better place in which to look for it. He found it too, it seems, in the shape of a beautiful peasant girl, to whom he became greatly attached as princes will, but whom he did not marry, as nowadays princes do. The sea far below us seemed unruffled in the still air and over on the horizon motionless cloud formations looked like unchartered enchanted islands.

We paused at Deyá, retreat of artists and Mr Robert Graves. It is a very small place, perched precariously on a protuberance from the mountain side. There seemed to be nobody about in its very small street, where we looked for some late breakfast. So we left Deyá a little crossly, as people do, when they do not find even a late breakfast, and continued on our way to Valldemosa.

There we were more successful and in the square under the walls of the monastery, we found all that was necessary for a late breakfast, including cold beer and a Majorcan delicacy, which was a kind of sweetened bread or pastry and is known as "prima" (meaning also "female cousin"). We ate it at a stall, to the sound of castanets and Spanish dance music coming from one of the buildings in the square. After a while the music ceased and abruptly there emerged from the building, tripping and laughing, a party of girls and children arrayed in white and dazzling the male observer with impressions of lace and kerchiefs and widely flouncing skirts. They were followed by a squad of men, grave by contrast in their black breeches, coloured waistcoats and Majorcan hats that reminded me somewhat of those once worn by Quakers.

We discovered that these people, dressed up in traditional Majorcan costume, which otherwise is no longer worn, had been giving a performance of Spanish dancing for a motor coach load of tourists.

Valldemosa is the plum of the island's tourist attractions, its cultural pearl, thought by travellers to be well worth a visit long before George Sand brought it notoriety. Now it is hallowed principally by her sojourn there with her lover whose illicit cohabiting, ironically enough, was held at the time to have desecrated the once sacred precincts of the monastery.

The Arabs, who gave it its beautiful name* were the first known to have appreciated the delights of Valldemosa. After their expulsion, the Majorcan King Sancho built his summer palace there and this was bequeathed in 1399 by King Martin to the Carthusians, an Order which seems to have a decided capacity for acquiring highly desirable properties in perfectly ideal surroundings.

The monks were still carrying out improvements in 1809 when Sir John Carr visited Majorca. They were then completing the decoration of the church,a process which involved a good deal of expenditure on gilt and skilled labour. As a result the funds of the monastery were at a low ebb and the monks felt obliged to spend less on hospitality. At the same time there was a sudden influx of brothers from the mainland, refugees from Barcelona, who more than doubled the number to be accommodated. An annoucement, inserted in the "Diario de Mallorca" soon after Carr's arrival in the island, stated that, owing to the arrival of "fifteen sons of St Bruno" from the continent and owing to the fact that more were expected, the *Hospederia* was being used as cells. The public were therefore asked not to visit the monastery until further notice. Carr refers to a similar annoucement in the "Palma Gazette" in which, he alleges, an exception to this ruling was made in favour of the English. Since the "Palma Gazette" did not exist at that time, it seems quite possible that the kind Majorcan gentlemen, who looked after Carr during his visit, may have told him about the notice in the "Diario de Mallorca", themselves adding an imaginary reference to the preferential treatment of the English, in order that the attractions of a visit to the monastery should be further enhanced by an aura of privilege. Carr's visit was in fact a success and the jolly fat prior, who had recently been entertained on a British man of war, was able to return the hospitality vicariously if slightly less lavishly, to the English knight.

But the days of conventual hospitality were already numbered and in 1835 it ceased when the monks of Valldemosa were expelled, as they were from other monasteries all over Spain. The deserted buildings were then sold to private persons. The former palace of King Sancho, which had been used by the monks as their guest house, was acquired by the Sureda family, while the three-roomed cells of the monastery proper became summer retreats for some of the wealthy citizens of Palma. It was in one of these cells or flats, as I suppose we ought now to call them, that the illustrious Spanish statesman and philosopher Jovellanos spent several years of his exile in Majorca, whither he had been sent by the spite of Godoy. This was before the monks were expelled and Jovellanos loved them and their monastery so well that, after he had been released from his six years of more rigorous confinement in Bellver Castle, his first action was to revisit Valldemosa. This occurred in 1808

*Said to be a corruption of the Arabic words "Vilayet" and "Mousa", meaning the domain of Mousa.

and the following year he was able to renew his discussions on the English Constitution with Lord Holland, whom he saw almost daily, dining, wining and visiting together the sights of Seville. It must have been a satisfactory reunion particularly for the Englishman, who five years previously had made strenuous efforts at the Spanish Court to secure his friend's release.

However it was not their great countryman's stay in Majorca that was most remembered at Valldemosa and in the Spanish edition of the pamphlet issued by the Direccion General de Turismo, his name was not even mentioned. (It was in the English edition.) Godoy's banishment of his person was evidently not considered adequate, I thought when I read the pamphlet; his memory must be banished as well. But this reflection was unjust, as I later discovered, for if Jovellanos was not featured at Valldemosa, he is at Bellver Castle, where the rooms he occupied are shown to visitors.

We had been introduced, if perfunctorily, to the Chopin/Sand saga, when, driving through France on our way to Majorca, we visited the Chateau de Nohant. There the souvenirs of Majorca so powerfully affected our three year old son that he had to be taken out to the garden with no better results. My diary records "He played with his car on G. Sand's tomb. Ann stopped him doing this." At Valldemosa no infantile outbursts disturbed the ethos of a place where no effort had been spared to impress the visitor with the importance of an author and her toy boy composer who stayed there more than a century ago. Memorabilia of this episode include the Pleyel piano she ordered from Paris for him which the Spanish customs did not release until shortly before he left. Photographs of virtuosos who had granted or been granted the privilege - one cannot be sure how they would feel about it - of striking a chord on it stared sternly down from their serried frames along the wall like a rostrum of Big Brothers on the lookout for any unseasonable flippancy in a pilgrim.

Other exhibits included a first edition of the book that inspired George Sand's visit, *Souvenirs d'un Voyage d'Art a l'Ile de Majorque* by the Provencal artist J.B. Laurens. We saw the manuscript of *Un Hiver à Majorque*, the book in which she had been so rude about the island and its inhabitants that a Spanish critic had recently censured the Majorcans for continuing to print it. Perhaps it would have been better if she had not come to Majorca so full of expectation not only from Laurens's book but from what she had been told by a distinguished Majorcan musician she had met in Paris, Don Francisco Frontera y la Serra, alias Valldemosa, who later became court musician to Queen Isabella. In her first letter written four days after her arrival at Palma Majorca was "la plus délicieuse résidence du monde" and this was despite the irritating *mucha calma* attitude not only of the locals but of the French consul towards her lodging arrangements. Later in the same letter, after poking fun at Majorcan carriages, she wrote of "Arab palaces, orange, lemon and palm trees, magnificent mountains, seas like a beautiful lake, delicious villages and an excellent population." She went on to write enthusiastically about her "cell" in the "immense and magnificent" charterhouse of Valldemosa with which she is "enchanted". In another letter a day later she wrote that Valldemosa was "the most romantic place in the world" and she "thinks she will never leave Majorca." And again, Valldemosa "is poetry, it is solitude, it is all that is most artistic ... what a sky, what countryside, we are in raptures" and yet again "the country, nature, the trees, the sky, the sea, the historic buildings exceed all my dreams. It is the promised land."

What more could she have said to express her delight in all she saw. Yet in her book she had hardly a good word and many bitter words to say of this "promised land". What could be the explanation for such a violent volte face? Robert Graves, in the introduction to his translation of her book, attempted to provide an answer to this question. With some plausibility he puts it all down to frustrated sex. He argues that her Catholic village neighbours, through the scheming of her jealous and malicious eight year old daughter, Solange, succeeded in reducing her relations with her lover to a strictly Platonic level. According to this theory, the threat of eternal damnation for his sinful life with George was so impressed upon an ailing and super-sensitive composer brought up in the Catholic faith that he was frightened temporarily out of his wits and permanently out of her bed.

Memorabilia were supported by a cast of custodians chosen apparently to look their part. The young man who languidly showed us the cell where Chopin may or may not have composed Preludes - his rooms have never been identified with certainty; I was told there were two houses in Valldemosa each with a room and a piano, both of which claimed to be the one in which the couple stayed - was pale, thin and of a melancholy countenance unrelieved by a bow tie. George Sand was represented by a middle-aged lady, managing, self-assured and French - a fair enough replica in the circumstances of the chatelaine of Nohant. The young women who ushered us solemnly from cell to cell behaved as if they were taking part in a ritual. It was a relief to arrive at last in the Prior's cell which was in the charge of a little fat Majorcan girl, who delighted us with her complete unawareness of the beauty and interest of the objects entrusted to her incurious care.

Each cell has a garden, enclosed on both sides by high walls, while the outer end coincides with the parapet of the great terrace wall of the monastery. These gardens which George Sand aptly described as "pretty drawing rooms of flowers" must be exactly like what they were in her day. Brilliant with flowers, shaded and scented by orange trees and cypresses, freshened by water running along stone irrigation channels, and with one end of it open to the sun-laden valley, each garden provided a rich banquet for the senses.

From the monastery proper we went to the former *Hospederia* or guest house, which had been occupuied as a private residence by the Sureda family, until the generosity with which they preserved its hospitable traditions brought them into financial difficulties and obliged them to give it up. Many distinguished people were among their guests. The American portrait painter John Singer Sargent when there in 1910 painted "Girls Gathering Blossoms". Other guests included the Spanish writers Azorín and Unamuno and the great Nicaraguan poet, Rubén Darío. The cell in which the latter slept is shown to visitors and the scarlet plush curtained bed creates an atmosphere appropriate to the ultra shades of the poet, who ended his life histrionically in the way he had lived it. He committed suicide attired in full evening dress and wearing a top-hat. On the wall of the cell hangs the text of his poem on the "Cartuja" (The Charterhouse), which displays those qualities of irresistible rhythm and brilliant colour of which Rubén Darío was so much the master. The theme of the poem is a rather too powerful contrast between the self-abnegation and continence of the monks and the self-indulgence and carnality of himself, the poet. His prayer to lead a life as virtuous as theirs is phrased a shade too passionately to be taken quite seriously.

*Darme otros ojos, no estos ojos vivos*
*Que gozan en miràr, como los ojos*
*De los satiros locos medio-chivos,*
*Redondeces de nieve y labios rojos.*

*Darme otra boca en que queden impresos*
*Los ardientes carbones del asceta,*
*Y no esta boca en que vinos y besos*
*Aumentan gulas de hombre y de poeta.*

*Darme unas manos de disciplinante*
*Que me dejen el lomo ensangrentado,*
*Y no estas manos lubricas de amante*
*Que acarician las pomas del pecado.*

*Darme una sangre que me deje llenas*
*Las venas de quietud y en paz los sesos*
*Y no esta sangre que have arder las venas,*
*Vibrar los nervios y crujir los huesos.*

Give me other eyes, not these lively
Eyes which enjoy looking, like the eyes
Of mad satyrs, semi-goats,
At snow white curves and scarlet lips.

Give me another mouth to which may be pressed
The burning coals of the ascetic
And not this mouth, which with wine and kisses
Excites the lusts of a man and a poet.

Give me the hands of a flagellant
Which will draw the blood from my back
And not these lubricious lover's hands
That caress the apples of sin.

Give me a blood that will leave the veins
Full of quietness and the brain in peace,
And not this blood which makes my veins burn,
My nerves vibrate and my bones creak.

No such sex-free yearnings would have troubled a later literary visitor to Valldemosa. While D.H. Lawrence was in Majorca thirteen of his pictures in an exhibition in London were considered so obscene by the Home Office that they were removed by the Police. Nevertheless sex could be sinful, as he insisted in a poem inspired by an encounter in a Palma tram:

### IN A SPANISH TRAMCAR

She fanned herself with a violet fan
and looked sulky, under the thick straight brows.

The wisp of modern black mantilla
made her half Madonna, half Astarte.

Suddenly her yellow-brown eyes looked with a flare into mine;
-we could sin together!-

The spark fell and kindled instantly on my blood,
then died out almost as swiftly.

She can keep her sin
She can sin with some thick-set Spaniard.
Sin doesn't interest me.

The dying Lawrence drove over to Valldemosa with his wife, Frieda, from Palma on 8 May 1929. He described the visit in a letter, dated "Ascension Day" to Aldous and Maria Huxley:

"Yesterday we motored to Valdemosa [*sic*], where Chopin was so happy and George Sand hated it. - It was lovely looking out from the monastery, into the dimness of the plain below, and the great loose roses of the monastery gardens so brilliant and spreading themselves out - then inside, the cloisters so white and silent. We picnicked on the north coast high above the sea, mountainous, and the bluest, bluest sea I ever saw - not hard like peacocks and jewels, but soft like blue feathers of the tit - really very lovely - and no people - olives and a few goats - and the big blueness shimmering to far off, north - lovely. Then we went on to Soller, and the smell of orange blossom so strong and sweet in all the air, one felt like a bee. - Coming back over the mountains we stopped in an old Moorish garden,* with round shadowy pools under palm trees, and big bright roses in the sun, and the yellow jasmine had shed so many flowers the ground was brilliant yellow - and nightingales singing powerfully, ringing in the curious stillness where the Moors have been, like ghosts - a bit *morne*, yet lovely for the time - like a pause in life. - It's queer, there is a certain loveliness about the island, yet a certain underneath ugliness, unalive."

From Valldemosa we returned to the coast road and continued along and up and down it through clouds of dust, past the meticulous terracings of Bañalbufar, until we came to the village of Estallenchs. From here we hoped to reach Camp de Mar by way of Andraitx, but an old man doddering by the roadside, seemed to imply by his gestures and something mumbled in Majorcan, that we could not do this. The owner of the pension at Estallenchs confirmed what the old man had tried to convey, explaining that the road had been blocked for some time past by repairs.

We therefore had to drive back half way to Valldemosa, and take the inland road via Puigpuñent. Though the day was hot and it was now certain that we should be very late for the luncheon that awaited us at Camp de Mar, we were not sorry that the repairs had been so drastic as to oblige us to return on our tracks. We had the road all to ourselves and did not meet another car until we arrived at Paguera. A profound pastoral peace brooded over the countryside and the lush vegetation of the narrow valley through which we were driving, proclaimed the existence of unusually plentiful supplies of water. Presently we caught sight of the great country house of Sa Granja, celebrated in Majorca for its fountains, springs and elaborate waterworks. It had at one time been possessed by a Moorish magnate and afterwards by the austere Carthusians, who were with difficulty persuaded to relinquish it in exchange for much less attractive premises in Palma. Their reluctance is not surprising. Conventual

* The reference to pools suggests this must have been Raxa.

life must be less irksome in a place where there are possibilities of and indeed inducements to communion with nature as well as with God and where the austerity of the cell may be relieved by "cheerful works beneath the sun".

Beyond Sa Granja the road winds over rounded hills planted with olives and then descends in hairpin bends so sharp that it was not possible to negotiate them without some extra manoeuvering.It had clearly not been designed for any great weight of traffic and Puigpuñent, when we reached it, seemed to be sunk in an overpowering lethargy brought on no doubt by sun, wine and isolation. A very old woman was the only human being visible and from her we asked the road to Paguera. We were having some difficulty in understanding her aged explanations and bewildered gesticulations when a youth appeared out of a deep hitherto unnoticed slumber and pointed the way. I think that if we had delayed a few more minutes we too would have quietly succumbed to the insidious mid-summer torpor of the place.

The road skirted the orchard slopes of Mount Galatzo, where Arago's bonfires in 1808 had excited the suspicions of a traditionally francophobe peasantry recently inflamed by the news of the Dos de Mayo, the day on which the people of Madrid rose in arms against the troops of Joseph Bonaparte. There is now a pension of excellent reputation situated high up on the hillside, historic also by its association with Jaime's campaign of conquest.

At Paguera we joined the main Palma road, which runs along the coast to Andraitx, and at once it seemed as if we were in another country. "Before you enter Palma you ought to visit the little port of Paguera," advised the French topographer, Alexandre de Laborde in 1809. Plenty of people do that today though usually after they have entered Palma and indeed the stretch of coastline between Palma and Andraitx is probably more frequented by tourists than any other part of Majorca, chiefly because of its proximity to Palma but also because it is sheltered from the North-Easterly winds that temper the heat of the northern shores of the island.

On emerging from the narrow dusty deserted road from Puigpuñent onto the shining metalled surface of the coast road with its busy traffic and smell of petrol fumes we left abruptly behind us the golden somnolence of the Isla de Calma and entered a more familiar world of hurry, noise and money. We seemed almost to have left the island for there was no longer a sense of remoteness, of being "away from it all"; we had the feeling rather of having returned suddenly to the continent, to some undeniably delicious resort, which had not quite escaped the taint of brash vulgarity that is brought along in the exhausts of a certain class of automobile.

It would be wrong however, to give even a slight impression that the Majorcan "Riviera" lacks charm. It has great charms, though they seemed not to be essentially Majorcan, but much more sophisticated, cosmopolitan and modern than one would expect from the island's real character, which is simple, inclined to be provincial and a little old-fashioned. The sophistication increases as you approach Palma and reaches its culmination in the vast hotels that struggle up the steep slopes of El Terreno and overlook the City and its famous Bay.

The entertainment we were given at Camp de Mar by Ann's wartime colleague Tomás Harris and his wife Hilda was equal to anything the French Riviera might offer and it had the additional savour often found only in the house of an artist. We arrived at a white stucco villa, bright with flowers and were led by a white-coated servant to our hostess on the terrace, where she had been awaiting us for at least an hour. She succeeded at once in making a virtue of our lateness and took us down to the private jetty, where we met our host, who had sensibly given us up, emerging from the pellucid waters of the bay. We in our turn slid into the same waters and then, invigorated by their cool caresses, returned up the slope to the terrace in keen anticipation of further refreshment internally from an ice-cold drink, or several. We were not disappointed and the next half hour or more was devoted to the sipping of champagne cocktails under the shade of a beach umbrella. The appetite having been adequately stimulated, there was an imperceptible move to the table, upon which a bowl of gazpacho, oleaginous, glistening, and scarlet struck a lively Spanish note. The note was not entirely Spanish, however, and the gazpacho not quite the austere dish as described by Richard Ford. There was no water in it and no bread but in exchange plenty of tomatoes, which were presumably unknown in Andalusia when Ford was gathering there. I have had the sort of gazpacho that he describes as "not easily digested by strangers" and am bound to say that I found the sophisticated version at the hospitable house at Camp de Mar a distinct improvement.

After lunch Tomás showed us round the house he was rebuilding in his garden to his own design. Next he gave us a demonstration of the manoeuvrability of his newly acquired three-wheeler midget car, one of the first to be seen in the island. Another had just reached Pollensa where it had aroused a mild interest chiefly among the members of the club who, on its arrival, had moved across the square in a body to examine it. We were spun one at a time with giddy-making virtuosity around Tomás's flower beds and then escorted by him triumphantly, past the hotel where Rudolf Valentino's widow once had reigned supreme as far as Paguera where we said good-bye, the richer not only by an experience of glamourous hospitality but also by the refilling of our empty wine jar from our host's butt.

Almost nine years later our lively and generous host was killed in a car accident in Majorca in circumstances thought by some to have been suspicious. Certainly if he had been driving his midget three-wheeler when the accident happened, he would have been especially vulnerable. *The Times* printed a tribute to him by another of his wartime colleagues, Sir Anthony Blunt, as he then was. Writing of his services when attached to the War Office Blunt recalled that "his special qualifications and his astonishing imagination enabled him to do work of the highest value to the Allied Cause, which won great commendation from those in high places who were in a position to judge it."

The house which Tomás was rebuilding had belonged to another British artist whose inspiration was remote from Tomás's. Whereas he was influenced by Spanish painters and in particular Goya, his predecessor at Camp de Mar, Cecil Aldin, was according to his *Times* obituarist in the great tradition of English sporting artists and a worthy successor of John Leech and Henry Alken. He had settled in Majorca in 1930 as the climate was thought to be good for his health. He suffered from rheumatoid arthritis aggravated if not caused by many falls in the hunting field.

Despite his infirmity he was able to continue drawing and painting animals, which in Majorca consisted solely of dogs. His English models which were brought out to Camp de Mar included a bull terrier named Cracker who, according to his proud owner, adored and was adored by Anna May Wong. To his English pack Aldin added an Ibizan hound which he claimed was one of the world's most ancient breeds. Unlike his English dogs Don Quixote, as he named it, was unmoved by the threat of a brandished riding crop. In Majorca dogs were brought to heel or stopped from chasing sheep by a well aimed stone. In this way the islanders preserved their primeval skill as slingers.

In his autobiography *Time I Was Dead* published the year before his death in 1935 he wrote that the Majorcans did not have much use for dogs or anyone interested in them. He recalled how incredulous a charming señorita had been when told he painted dogs. When assured it was true she exclaimed "No comprendo, Señor, why paint dogs?" She evidently knew less about the English than the Emperor Charles V who spoke their language to his dogs.

Aldin, the life-long fox hunter, wrote dispassionately and knowledgeably of bull fighting but, though he was not blind to its drama and though he admired the courage of bull fighters, he had no doubt it was cruel especially to horses. To illustrate the difference between the English and the Spanish attitude to bull fighting he told a story of an English lady who wanted to start a branch of the R.S.P.C.A. in Palma. Having been advised that she should seek the support of a high town official, she went to see him and was sympathetically received. When she agreed with him that money would be necessary to start the project, he told her that a bull fight could easily be arranged as a fund raiser.

Many years later an English lady did start an affiliate of the R.S.P.C.A. in Palma but without help from the bullring. Mary Louise Paxman was born at Stisted Hall, Essex, the daughter of a successful engineer whose firm still flourishes at Colchester, of which he was several times Mayor. A beautiful and determined young woman, she fell in love with an Australian Army officer while on a two day voyage from Algeciras to Marseilles, married him soon afterwards and left with him for Australia. When one of their children fell ill Jane, as she became known, returned to England with her husband, Clement Gladstone ("Toby") Reynolds, who transferred to the British Army. After his retirement as a Brigadier in 1955 they went to live in Majorca for his health. They bought a piece of land at Paguera where they built a house which the Brigadier, being an engineer, designed.

Almost at once Jane and Toby became active in the Sociedad Protectora de Animales y Plantas into which they breathed new life. Jane raised funds from the expatriate colony, recruited staff and arranged for an inspection by and affiliation to the R.S.P.C.A. while Toby built new animal pens and designed a crematorium. All this activity appears to have upset some of the Spanish members of the Sociedad's governing body and when Jane and her husband were on a visit to England she and other expatriates on it were expelled. It may have been some consolation to the Reynolds when, in recognition of their "10 years love and care for destitute animals in Mallorca", their "grateful admirers" presented them in April 1970 with a group of silver statuettes of a horse and two dogs.

Less than a year later Toby died, Jane sold their house at Paguera, moved to a flat at Santa Ponsa and, as a seventy year old widow, founded another refuge for destitute animals the Centro Canino Internacional. Premises were acquired at No. 71 Calle Jesus near the centre of Palma and there year after year until the day of her death Jane Reynolds, assisted by a paid staff of two Majorcans, looked after every day an average of 300 animals, mostly cats and dogs. The Centro was affiliated from the start with the R.S.P.C.A., which supported it with cash and equipment including a van which delivers the

Centro's supply of drinking water. The Centro receives support not only from the Anglo-Saxon colony and other expatriates in the island but from the islanders themselves. For example the Deputy Mayor of Palma has given his official backing to the Centro and its President, Sr Alfonso Salgado, whose wife is English, is a former member of the Balearic Parliament. Above all, the Centro most depends on its honorary vet, Don Pedro Murell who for years has given his services free.

After Jane Reynolds died on 4 July 1991, aged eighty-nine, the Centro she had founded and to which she had given the last eighteen years of her long life, was named in her honour The Jane Reynolds Foundation. Two years before she died she showed what stuff she was made of when threatened with imprisonment. In a fit of socialist absurdity a Spanish authority fined her the equivalent of £600 for not paying a local inhabitant to do what she did at the Centro voluntarily for nothing. She refused to pay the fine, being quite prepared to go to prison particularly as she understood the Palma dungeons were unusually comfortable. In the end the authority came to its senses, no fine was paid and Jane did not go to prison.

******

Valldemosa, by virtue of its associations with international celebrities as well as its easy accessibility from Palma, will no doubt always be a bigger attraction for tourists than Lluch is ever likely to be, and precisely for that reason the smaller and less well known monastery will continue to have a special charm. We drove there one day early in April by a road that is among the most beautiful of the many beautiful roads in Majorca. It runs first through the narrow fertile valley of March, whose green meadows, sparkling streamlets, neat orchards and handsome farmhouses gave an impression of such delicious plenty that it seemed as if it must enjoy the special protection of a benignant God; as if Ceres herself had chosen it for a model estate.

At the other end of this valley the road climbs up into the mountains and we were soon driving through a country of bare grey rock, the sort of country of which Vulcan might have been the absentee landlord. Gustave Doré's illustrations for "The Inferno" were said to have been inspired by this shattered landscape, but though the artist certainly toured Spain in 1862 with his friend and patron, the great antiquarian, Baron Charles Davilier, it is now considered improbable that he also accompanied him to Majorca. His drawings of Majorcan scenery have an indeterminate quality, which suggest that they were not based on his own observation but at second-hand on descriptions, and perhaps sketches, provided by the Baron. Nevertheless local legend still maintains that Doré worked at 'Sa Coma', near Valldemosa.

A notice board indicating a Spanish Government Experimental Farm announced the beginning of a less hellish region and almost immediately we were descending into the pleasant little purgatory in which the monastery of Lluch is situated. It is approached by an avenue of plane trees and a bridge over the mountain torrent that runs along the east front, whose austere architecture, a little too evocative of sack-cloth and workhouses, might momentarily daunt the ardent pilgrim. We drove over the bridge, under an archway and found ourselves in the forecourt of the monastery, a long rectangle flanked by low buff buildings which include a shop, a somewhat unenticing cafe and an assortment of coach houses, cow sheds and stables. The high and unelaborate facade of the monastery occupies one end of the square and at the top of a flight of steps the main door stood open urging the stranger to enter. We did so and were greeted by a well-fed cleric whose plump pink countenance shone with benevolent shrewdness and who proved a well-informed guide.

We were shown first the guests' refectory or dining room for, by contrast with the monastery's harsh exterior, only a slightly bare simplicity distinguished it from an ordinary restaurant. It looks onto a garden, whose luxuriant sub-tropical vegetation almost fills the quadrangle and somehow recalls, with its air of studied abandonment, Kinglake's famous description of the gardens of Damascus. In the inner courtyard there is a statue of a bishop and a couple of very ancient motor cars, whose snub noses were pressed against the wall of the chapel like two jolly dunces being disciplined under the episcopal eye. The interior of the chapel is agreeably gaudy and notable for the local marble employed in its construction. Behind the apse there is a special chamber which contains a Virgin famous for the miracle she is said to have wrought. I asked our reverend guide if there had been any recent examples of her miraculous powers. He made a slight deprecatory gesture, the scarcely perceptible twitch of one who would like to shrug his shoulders but who thinks it prudent not to. The question was clearly one he would have preferred not to have to answer. He told us, however, of an occurrence widely held to rank as a miracle. Not long ago a builder working on the fourth floor which was being added to some of the monastery buildings, had slipped and fallen to the ground and, to the amazement of the on-lookers, had picked himself up unharmed. With a look, which seemed to say you can take it or leave it, the priest dismissed the story and I am still wondering whether to take it.

The Museum, which was our next stopping place, called forth an enthusiastic commentary from its fond guardian. Our expressions of mild though genuine interest provoked torrents of information, and the flood did not cease with the particular object of our curiosity but poured comprehensively and piously over vestments and scapularies, pieces of jewellery and pieces of plate, crucifixes and rosaries, missals and breviaries, so that we began to feel quite drowned in the flood of iconographical detail.

It was a relief to come down to a more practical level, when we moved from the museum to the guest rooms, which turned out to be both austere and comfortable. Tiled floors of immaculate cleanliness, beautiful furniture, a crucifix, a cubicle containing a wash basin and - profane apparatus - a bidet, nothing was omitted that could contribute to a pilgrim's spiritual and physical refreshment. Even cooking facilities were provided, if needed, all at a cost of less than 25p a day per person (N.B. in 1955!). Yet I believe not one of the rooms was occupied, though later in the year they are all taken, chiefly by citizens of Palma.

Originally an Augustinian foundation dating from 1430, a century later the monastery was taken away from that order, possibly because of lapses in discipline, and converted into a choir school which it has remained to this day. It is now staffed by some ten priests and there are approximately fifty senior students and a hundred children. The latter are nicknamed "Blauets" from the blue garments they wear like the boys of another famous school in another island. We did not see much evidence of these students or children and the monastery was as quiet and seemed as empty as the Theatine school at Pollensa. In this respect our experience was different from that of a pious and high spirited young lady who visited the monastery with her Uncle and Aunt on 4th May 1890, having ridden there on muleback from Soller through scenery which was the finest she had ever seen and stopping to "grub up a huge basketful of spray orchids". The priest in charge was most hospitable and they dined "in a huge dining hall" where they were waited on by "two of the College boys, dear and jolly little chaps". In those days "anybody, stranger or otherwise, could sojourn there for three days, without payment, being provided with beds, damp sheets, salt, olives, oil and bread, but on condition that you bring all other necessaries in the way of food." The La Trobe Bateman party were made especially welcome by their host, who was no doubt well aware of the importance of his guests and his hospitality became almost abandoned when he sent to their table "a bottle of Old Tom! Of all things in the world (which greatly astonished us)". The priest begged them to use his own quarters which "had a decided idea of comfort" but they preferred to "fare as other folk". Not quite as other folk perhaps for "they were extremely comfortable ... of course having Margarita with us made a great difference in every way."

The next morning the La Trobe Batemans continued on muleback until they came to a village where, much to Mildred's relief, they were met by their groom, Antonio with the carriage and borne home to their "dear little shanty" at La Puebla. We left Lluch by car, which like Margarita of course made a great difference, and enabled us to have a picnic on the top of the pass on the road from Lluch to Inca. The choice of a picnic site can seldom have been made with such unanimous spontaneity. Such choices are made more often than not out of sheer desperation by the man at the wheel after the remainder of the party have failed to agree on previous and better possibilities and when everyone's tempers have been frayed by hunger and argument. But on this occasion it was clear at once to all that we had arrived at a spot, which might have been designed by nature for the ideal picnic on that day. From it there was a magnificent view, for the whole of the Majorcan plain seemed to be stretched out below us. We were sheltered by a low rock wall from the breeze, which at that altitude, even on that sunny day, in a Majorcan April was just fresh enough to make shelter from it desirable. So we sat down in a rocky alcove and ate Francisca's cold fried fish and drank bottles of vino tinto with the sun above us and the world at our feet.

The road down from the pass is beautifully engineered, like every mountain road in Majorca, all the experience of generations of terrace makers having gone into it. These terraces, which climb up the mountain side on the steepest and most marginal slopes, became broader and greener as we descended into the valley and approached the first village, Selva. This is notable for the festivals of folk dancing, which are held there once a week for tourists. The large parish church was the scene of an embarrassing incident in the life of one of Majorca's greatest men. Fray Junípero Serra, the Apostle of the Golden Province, was in the middle of one of his celebrated Lenten sermons, when a lady in the congregation, driven to a frenzy by his impassioned eloquence, grew beside herself and cried out in a loud voice "Yell away, yell away, but you will not see the end of Lent!" This must have been disconcerting at the time but years later in the wilds of California, the good priest recalled the incident with nostalgic amusement.

\*\*\*\*\*\*

It was not long after our arrival at the Villa that Francisca first told us about market day at Inca. The market was held every Thursday, in fact it had been held on that day for at least a century and probably much longer. Francisca, who never tired of trying to devise ways and means of housekeeping with the maximum economy, urged us to visit the market and lay in a good supply of provisions, which we should be able, she assured us, to buy more cheaply than at the Puerto or at Pollensa. She suggested further that Fernando should accompany us, as he knew what prices should be paid and where the best value was to be obtained. One Thursday morning therefore, we set off for Inca, with Fernando to direct operations.

On entering the town, it at once became apparent that market day at Inca was no ordinary market day. Our further progress by car was barred by a Guardia Civil, who told us that the whole of the centre of the town was closed to traffic in the interests of the market. Entire streets, we soon found, were devoted to the sale of a particular produce, which was displayed on the pavements and in the roadway. Crowds of chickens, heaps of potatoes, artichokes, cabbages and lettuces, sacks of rice, chick peas and lentils, pots and pans, cloth and clothes, lined the streets in bewildering profusion. The main square too, was overflowing with all manner of vegetables and the space between each stall was so narrow and the customers so numerous, that it was difficult to move. The hot sun beat strongly down on the sweating, jostling crowds and as we struggled with our heavily laden baskets we began to doubt whether the economies we were undoubtedly making were not being paid for too highly.

It was a relief to return to the Bodega, where we had left our garafa (a bulbous bottle with a narrow neck containing eight litres) to be replenished with red wine from Binisalem. The Bodega was a vast cellar-like room, which you entered by a rough doorway and a flight of steps leading down from one of the streets off the square. The walls were lined with immense casks which must have measured at least ten feet in diameter. The room was crowded with people seated at tables and eating steaming savoury-smelling food. Their rustic clothing, the rough tables covered with a coarse crockery and cutlery, the dark wood of the casks and the dim light, for there were no windows, imparted a somewhat sombre medieval atmosphere to the place, which contrasted powerfully with the bright liveliness of the chaffering streets.

Having completed our marketing and piled high the car with provender, we had no energy left to visit the porcelain factory with Fernando, who had promised earlier in the day to act as guide. He did not remind us of his offer and after such an expense of effort in bargaining and elbowing and carrying, no doubt was relieved that we did not mention it. We ought, however, to have visited the factory, since Inca has been credited with the distinction of having first manufactured what afterwards became widely known as Majolica. The connexion between Majorca and Majolica was until recently thought to be so indirect as to make the derivation of the word uncertain. The theory was that the Tuscan potters, who copied the process of iron glazing used in Hispano-Moorish ceramics, called their new ware Majolica, not because the original came from Majorca, but because it was brought from Spain to Italy in Majorcan ships. However a discovery made by the Marchesa Origo in the Datini archives at Prato now shows that there was a better reason for the name and puts its derivation beyond doubt. In 1390 the "Merchant of Prato" received from Valencia a dinner service which he liked so much that he asked his agents there to send him another for use in his house at Florence. The agents failed to carry out his instructions and the Merchant eventually had the new dinner service made in Majorca, quite possibly by the craftsmen of Inca. Thus it would seem that Majolica was so named, not merely because it came in Majorcan ships, but because it was originally manufactured in Majorca.

When Sir John Carr visited Inca, "he was conducted by a monk to the only place worthy of notice, the nunnery of Santa Gerona, where one of the sisters played most execrably upon the organ, after which we were conducted to a window and regaled with the sight of the corpse of one of the nuns who had been dead several years and appeared to be in a high state of ghastly preservation." The remains were still to be seen when Gaston Vuillier visited the church nearly eighty years later, when their state of preservation must have been considerably "higher". Having been delayed one afternoon at Inca we decided to investigate this convent, for it is true that there is in the town not much that is of particular architectural or historical interest. What Carr referred to as Santa Gerona is in fact the convent of San Geronimo. No doubt he misunderstood what was told him and there were then no guide books from which he could check the spelling. Indeed to this day (1955) there appears to be no guide or potted history of Inca, though it is the third most important town in Majorca.

We eventually located the convent at the top of a steep hill some distance from the market place. The road ended in a roughly paved courtyard, one side of which consisted of a number of cottages at whose doors some fat old women were busy in gossip. One of them offered to show us the church, whose south wall formed an arcade along another side of the courtyard. The interior of the church was lined, like the church at Lluch, with black local marble and was excessively dark. We found neither organist nor corpse, the latter possibly having become too ghastly for inspection in our sensitive age. The embalmed body of King Jaime II used also to be on view in Palma Cathedral, but a tip to one of the Canons will no longer obtain for the curious tourist a sight of the royal relics. At the back of the church a heavily barred aperture in the wall enabled one to peer into the blackness beyond. It was from here presumably that the nuns were able to witness the public celebration of mass. We emerged once more into the sunlight and listened to what little the old woman could tell us about the convent, how it was founded about 1405, to replace a nunnery in the mountains, which had been abandoned, and how the church was formerly the parish church of Inca.

******

If anyone asked me what I liked best about Palma, I do not think that I should say the Cathedral or the Bay or the Lonja or the Almudaina but the Borne. One of the most celebrated streets of Europe, it was renamed Avenida Generalissimo Franco but continued to be known locally by its original name. Our first and our last impressions of Majorca were of the Borne. The first when early in the morning of our arrival we sipped delicious chocolate and ate ensaimadas at the Cafe Formentor and on the evening of our departure when we dined at the Oriente and were entertained by the conversation of the waiter. This genial person boasted of having remained a bachelor until well into his forties, a feat that must be unique in the annals of the Greater Aphrodisiad; but he was paying for it now with a rapidly increasing family. His brother, possibly with the idea of escaping a similar fate, had taken up permanent residence in London.

To be a cafe lounger, if the Borne were to be your beat, would surely be the ideal career for any man of inaction. The Borne has everything that the most exacting cafe lounger could require. It has warmth and sunshine, the shade of noble trees, a broad promenade displaying uniforms and pretty dresses, pretty figures and pretty faces,* and desultory traffic including agreeable trams, which CLANG complainingly by, recalling the golden days of cafe lounging, when solitary gentlemen of modest means could afford at an early age to retire to the sun.

Naturally if you are a confirmed and arrant cafe lounger, you will never leave the shaded water-sprinkled pavement of the Borne, but if you are something less than that and have inelegantly energetic peripatetic tendencies, you will occasionally leave your cafe table and take a stroll around the streets and squares that lie on both sides of the Borne. Your exertions will be amply rewarded for you will find in these quiet, narrow, crooked streets, not perhaps glamour and romance, but an ineffable placidness that is refreshing to those whose lives are led in the noise and smell of more turbulent thoroughfares. Through broad flat archways one can catch glimpses of delightful patios ablaze with flowers.

Much has been made of the so-called Moorish atmosphere of these streets of old Palma. This, I think, has been exaggerated by those who would like to see in the Palma of Jaime the Conqueror, traces of the Moorish city upon whose ruins it was built. Hilaire Belloc, rejoicing perhaps a little provocatively at the triumph won for Christendom by Jaime, wrote that there was "an effect of Barbary on the place" and that it was "all indefinably touched with something of the eastern past; far less than Africa, but more than Sicily". So indefinable, I think, that it may not exist. Havelock Ellis too says, "The first and perhaps the most abiding impression made by Palma is its Moorish aspect" and again "I know no city in Christendom which so subtly suggests the persistence of Moorish influence." So subtle indeed that Havelock Ellis admits, "it might escape a visitor who is not familiar with Morocco." Too subtle for me who finds nothing in common between Fez for example and Palma, beyond the fact that they are both ancient capitals with narrow tortuous streets. In other respects they seem to me to be totally dissimilar. Nobody who had ever smelt the stench of Fez would lightly compare it with immaculate Palma, whose walls and houses are built of stone, while those of Fez are built of mud. There is not even in Palma a great monument surviving from the Golden Age of Moorish civilization as there are in Granada, Seville and Cordoba where, if anywhere, nostalgia for a ruined culture may surely most effectively be indulged. All that remains in Palma of Moorish architecture are some subterranean baths and possibly traces of Moorish influence in the slender columns that support many a Gothic archway.

But the main thing after all about Palma is not its Moorish nor its Spanish nor its Catalan atmosphere, but the fact that it is the first Majorcan city, both in date and in importance, the capital of an ancient kingdom which, though

---

*In *El Paisaje de España* Azorín wrote eloquently of "esta belleza de Mallorca" he encountered in the streets of Palma.

united after a comparatively short period of independence with the crown of Aragon and later of Spain, has nevertheless preserved, as probably only an island could in the circumstances, its own identity. The excellence and variety of its hotels, shops and restaurants, the cleanness and elegance of its streets, the apparent - and I believe real - absence of extreme poverty, the deference paid to the arts, the friendliness of its inhabitants and their ability to live without that "sick hurry" which afflicts more northern people - "mucha calma" meaning "take it easy" is Majorca's watchword - make a combination that will be found not only in Palma but to a greater, or lesser degree, in all the towns of Majorca and is much if not all of the island's character.

In any account of Palma it would, I suppose, be provoking not to mention either the Lonja or Bellver Castle, which are after the Cathedral, the two most notable buildings the city possesses. It would however be dishonest of me to pretend that I felt any great enthusiasm for them or that if I were to write at any length about them I should do anything more than copy, parrotwise, what has already been said about them by others. Perhaps I should have felt differently about the Lonja, if we had been able to get inside it but it was locked when we tried and as it was raining hard, we did not try for long,* but took shelter in the Bahia Palace Hotel nearby, an outré erection of concrete and chromium plate financed by the Society of Jesus. The Lonja is nevertheless a worthy testimony of the past mercantile glories of Palma, which rivalled even those of Venice, and the Bahia Palace is equally a fitting tribute to the sources of much of her present wealth.

As for Bellver Castle, some see it as the Majorcan Windsor Castle, others as the local Bastille and all would be right as it has been both in its time. Built by Jaime II of Majorca for the defence of the newly founded city of Palma, enjoyed by John II of Aragon as a retreat in which to pursue his amorous enterprises, it finally became a place for the detention of political undesirables, of whom Jovellanos was the most famous. An inscription on the walls of one of the dungeons and a plaque inserted in the wall of the courtyard records or used to record, the fate of one of his forgotten contemporaries, General Luis Lacy.

One of the better Spanish generals, who fought alongside the British in the Peninsular War, Lacy was a constant companion of General Graham when they were both at Cadiz. Their friendship came to an abrupt end after the battle of Barrosa Heights, when Graham challenged Lacy to a duel unless he withdrew some insulting observations in a pamphlet, giving the Spanish version of the events which caused the battle to be only a partial if not a pyrrhic victory. Lacy withdrew the observations and General Graham returned to England to found the Senior United Services Club, to breed prize cattle and to die many years later at the ripe old age of ninety-seven. No such peaceful retirement awaited his former friend and comrade in arms. An ardent believer in constitutional government, General Lacy led the revolt in Catalonia against the repression of Ferdinand VII. The revolt was crushed by Lacy's old enemies, the French, and he himself, after enduring in Bellver Castle starvation and the black squalor of an oubliette, was taken out and shot.

A more fortunate inmate of the castle was the great French scientist Arago, whose adventures in Majorca have formed the subject of one of several Franco-Majorcan controversies, to which George Sand's visit to the island has

*I did visit it many years later and admired the interior.

given rise. Arago was sent on a scientific mission to Spain by the French Government in 1806 with another French scientist and a Spanish *commissary* named Rodriguez. Their task, which had already been begun by a third Frenchman who had died, was to prolong the meridional line as far as the island of Formentora. Arago and Rodriguez left Spain for Majorca early in 1808 and, though England and France were at war, the Royal Society procured for the French scientist a safe conduct from the Admiralty so that he should be able to pass unmolested if his ship were intercepted by a British cruiser, an arrangement of such magnanimity as to be unthinkable in our more suspicious times.

Having arrived safely in Majorca, Arago took his station on the top of Mount Galatzo and got on with his job. In the meantime the popular uprising against the French after the Dos de Mayo had broken out and the effigies of prominent persons, including the Majorcan born finance minister Soler, who were known to be partisans of Godoy and the French, were being burnt by an infuriated mob in the streets of Palma. Arago, however, was left undisturbed until popular suspicion and indignation were aroused by an unfortunate incident. This was the arrival at Palma on May 27th 1808, of a French officer with orders for the Spanish squadron at Port Mahon to proceed to Toulon. He could hardly have come at a worse moment, for two days later the Supreme Junta was set up in Majorca with the avowed policy of joining England in the war against France.

As soon as the purpose of the French officer's mission became known to the populace, putting two and two together, took it into their heads that the fires, which Arago had to light on Mount Galatzo in connexion with his work, were in reality signals for communicating with the French fleet. Having made up their minds that the unfortunate scientist was nothing less than an enemy agent in disguise, a party of wrathful security-minded citizens sallied forth to execute summary justice. Arago however received warning of their approach from the master of the sailing ship that had been put at his disposal by the Spanish Government. This brave man dressed Arago up as a seaman and in this garb the scientist, who met the angry posse on their way up the mountain, was able to tell them in fluent Mallorquin where the Frenchman was not to be found.

Much of the foregoing and the story of how Arago was subsequently taken into protective custody in Bellver Castle is recounted by George Sand in "Un Hiver à Majorque". She relates too how a monk attempted to poison him and it is this accusation that has been challenged by Majorcan historians, who consider that the Majorcan authorities acted with considerable courage in protecting Arago and also the French courier from the fury of the mob. There does seem to be some truth nevertheless in the poisoning story. George Sand states that Arago had promised to write his version of these events and years later he did so in an autobiographical sketch, "The History of My Youth", an English translation of which by the Rev. Mr Baden Powell appeared in 1855.

According to this account the Spanish governor of the castle himself, whose confidence Arago had won by listening sympathetically to his theories on the efficiency of water as a panacea, told the tactful prisoner of the plot to poison him. When shortly afterwards the devoted Rodriguez, the Spanish commissary, the only person who still dared to visit him in daylight, brought him a copy of a newspaper describing in advance his courageous and dignified bearing at his execution, Arago decided that even Bellver Castle was no longer a safe retreat.

Accordingly he obtained the permission of the Captain General, Luis Vives, to "escape" and after many vicissitudes, he and the French courier got safely back to France.

We were content to observe the great bulk of Bellver from afar. Its attractions were not strong enough to persuade us to traverse the noisy suburb of El Terreno in order to go inside. More appealing somehow than this disused donjon with its stale memories of royal merry-making and jailer's brutalities are some of Palma's buildings that are still living and contributing to the essential atmosphere of the Greater Aphrodisiad. Chief among these is the magnificent market, in which there is to be found a wonderful profusion of the good things of the earth at the cheapest prices in the island. Palma market is of comparatively recent construction and it affords evidence of the great progress in agriculture that the Majorcans, in spite of their intense conservatism, have achieved in the last hundred years. This progress, which has been in scope rather than in methods, is well illustrated by a comparison between the limited range of locally grown vegetables to be had in the 1860's and the infinite variety available today. Consul Bidwell complained that "beetroot, artichokes,\* turnips, seakale, cucumber, and several useful vegetables known in England ... are literally unknown in the market; not because they could not be readily grown to great perfection but because it is simply out of the groove as yet to cultivate them." But now all these things and many more are to be had in plenty.

The great improvements in Majorcan agriculture effected during the nineteenth century were due firstly to the work of the Sociedad Econòmica de los Amigos del País, secondly to the removal of certain customs legislation, which discouraged any progress whatever in any branch of Majorcan life, and thirdly to the introduction of new ideas by French refugees during the Revolution. No account of Majorca, however superficial, ought to omit a brief description of the Sociedad Econòmica. It was founded in 1778 by a number of enlightened and patriotic Majorcan noblemen and gentlemen with the object of stimulating improvements in trade and industry, education and culture and indeed in every field of Majorcan life except the Church, for which the members of the Sociedad continued to profess unlimited respect, even when she was guilty of the most outrageous absurdities. The Sociedad founded art and technical schools, encouraged education for women, introduced new methods of agriculture, established new industries, gave prizes for art, agriculture and industry and assisted the French refugees, of whom there were as many as 3,000 to turn to the best advantage the specialised knowledge and skill that many of them had brought with them; like that admirable Canon from Albi who introduced improved methods for brandy distilling.

The Sociedad's schemes for improvement were discussed and advertised in its weekly "Palma de Mallorca", which was the first periodical to be published in the Island. As a result of this introduction and circulation of fresh ideas and the enthusiastic support given to experiments in agriculture and industry, the last two decades of the eighteenth century saw a miniature cultural and economic renaissance in Majorca, which fell into a decline with the financial stringency caused by the Napoleonic wars and died under the withering repression of Ferdinand VII.

\*Henry Christmas however, writing in 1851, saw artichokes which were "Inferior to the English variety".

Nevertheless the work of the Sociedad had not by any means been in vain and much that is useful and productive in Majorca today owes its origins to its enlightened energy. Traces of it may be seen in Palma in the two glass factories, which form a large proportion of the island's blessedly small industrial wealth. One of these glassworks is situated near the city walls in an ancient cavernous building, and in this respect it is scarcely a model factory. Indeed the scene as you enter recalls an engraving of a Victorian factory, as depicted by a zealous reformer. The gloom of the place, when we visited it was hardly relieved by a few electric bulbs, while at intervals the pale and sweating faces of the workers, who seemed to include boys and old men, were lit up in the white hot glow of a furnace. We watched them transforming lumps of molten amber-coloured glass, like barley sugar, into most realistic bulls, swiftly and deftly drawing out their protuberances with a pair of tweezers, which they wielded with amazing virtuosity. They kindly gave us several of these creations and also some amber crocodiles with inordinately long tails, all the while keeping a watchful look-out for the boss, who presumably would have preferred us to buy his wares, if we were to acquire any of them at all.

For the proper appreciation of Majorcan rancidness - or rancidity - it is essential to visit the house of Guasp, which must be one of the oldest bookselling and printing establishments in the world. The woodcuts, that may be seen in the Guasp museum, depicting the Majorcan hagiarchy, illustrate better perhaps than other art forms, the benign but occasionally ferocious bigotry of the islanders - though this may well have been exaggerated and is probably on the decline. It is unlikely that the modern Majorcan would attribute some natural disaster such as a protracted drought to the machinations of the heretic English as their grandfathers are said to have done. Even in our brief experience of the island we encountered signs, if not of scepticism, of a certain luke-warmness. It had come as a surprise for example, when our servants declined our offer to transport them to mass on Easter Day, "as it would be too crowded," they said. On the western side of the island, notably at Andraitx, I was told the people were very anti-clerical. Since they were mostly staunch republicans they associated priests with the Franco regime.

What is conceivably typical of Majorca may be savoured at the Museo Luliano, not in it but in the patio, which basks so beautifully in the sun that you may not get as far as the museum, which in any case is sure to be shut. Then there is the State Library in the Calle Montesion, where eighteenth century scholarship moulders quietly on worm-eaten shelves, surmounted by carven heads, which peer pop-eyed into the dim light of the great musty room. The sunlit patio and the worm-eaten library, each was suggestive of two Majorcan essentials, the abundant lust for life and the somewhat slow-moving silt-laden stream down which a history of peaceful uninterrupted habit has caused it to flow.

Whether the immense irruption of foreigners into Majorca during the last seventy years is likely to burst the banks of this pleasant stream and lead to disagreeable inundations over alien fields or even to a total diversion into less placid channels, is a matter for speculation. Hilaire Belloc wrote, "I have heard for these thirty years past that the special soul of Palma can not survive, that it is with everyday more visited and becoming from a thing, a name. I expected when I revisited it to find it half ruined," but after twenty-one years he found that Palma had lost less than any other of the towns he knew. Another seventy years have gone by since Belloc was in Palma and the tourist trade has vastly increased during that time. Belloc had not seen the Bahia Palace. Yet, I think, after what I have seen and heard during several recent visits, he would still feel confident that Palma, and therefore Majorca, would remain a place "in which tradition is alive and beauty preserved without effort, without archaism, without affectation; but as part of a continued life." This may make the people "dullish" as a great contemporary of Belloc's found them, but it has enormous charm for the visitor from the more urgent, if more progressive north.

# CHAPTER V
# SOME PEOPLE

*Missionary; Revolutionary; Afrancesado; Liberal*

No profound historical considerations have influenced, as will be apparent, my choice of the four personalities who form the subjects of this chapter. They were not selected, for example, to illustrate the Majorcan character nor to support any generalizations about the nature of Majorcan social, religious and economic life. To do this it would be necessary at least to examine in full the life and work of Raymond Lull and to analyse the extraordinary veneration in which the Majorcans hold Saint Catalina Tomas, that somewhat priggish and sanctimonious peasant girl, whose biography by Cardinal Despuig has been a best seller in Majorca since its publication in 1816.

My choice has been governed partly by chance and partly by curiosity. I was led by chance to the names of Picornell, Cladera and Bauza about whom I was curious to know more and to that of Junípero Serra because of his connection with things that are familiar. Serra founded California, Picornell began the liberation of Spanish America, Cladera translated an English classic and Bauza received - my friend the Palma archivist told me - the Order of the Garter. Obscure though they may be to a person unacquainted with Majorcan history, as I was when I first heard of them, they are nevertheless slightly illuminated in the glare of world history, if only after numerous reflections. They therefore lend themselves to be displayed more readily to the general reader than those worthies who are completely hidden in the remote fastnesses of the island's chronicles.

## *MISSIONARY*

There are some people whose lives may be known only by their deeds. Anyone who is completely dedicated to a single purpose to the extent that selfish desires and considerations are utterly suppressed is likely to furnish a biographer with meagre and dull material. For the most diverting parts of a biography are precisely those which are concerned with the subject's passions, personal opinions and prejudices, whims and oddities, and their impact on other people. A Life of the Duke of Wellington would make tedious reading for the civilian reader if there were nothing more to it than a series of military campaigns, if there were no tales of smashed violins and smashed windows, of pretty married ladies and pious single ones, of pungent outbursts of personality in court and camp.

The life of the founder of California, at any rate as it is presented in the pages of his friend, fellow missionary, fellow countryman and first biographer, Father Francisco Palou is dull as biography because once it has been said that Fray Junípero dedicated himself body and soul to the evangelisation of the pagan tribes of Mexico, all the rest is mere repetition. There is no weakening, no letting up, no deviation of purpose, no doubts and no regrets. Even disappointments and setbacks lose their meaning because they are transmuted into expressions of the Will of God. There are no recriminations, spites, jealousies, quarrels nor reconciliations, which furnish whole volumes for students of sinners and ordinary men, for in Fray Junípero's human as well as his divine relations, all bad feelings melted, as it were, in the fierce glow of his universal

71

charity. Only perhaps in his affection for his two fellow labourers from Majorca, Fathers Palou and Crespi, is it possible to discern a slight human weakness, an almost rueful admission to a preference.

Allowance must of course be made for the probability that Father Palou may have magnified his friend's virtues and kept silent about his weaknesses, no doubt unconsciously, in the hope that the shining example of the revered missionary would further the cause which they both had so much at heart. Yet when due allowance has been made both for the exaggerations of propaganda and also for Father Palou's somewhat limited qualifications as a biographer, Fray Junípero Serra's life is an extraordinary record of heroism and single-minded devotion to an ideal. He was born at Petra on 24th November, 1713, into a humble peasant family. The house in which he is believed to have lived as a child is now preserved as a place of historic interest and may be visited by the public. One morning early we drove from Palma to see Petra. We had been at the airport, where we talked to the airport chaplain, whom we had previously met in a Palma street, when we had asked him the way. On this occasion we found him seated on a bench contemplating perhaps his, to us, in all respects, nebulous functions. In the course of our brief encounters with him he had appeared to us a man of much simple charity and intelligence, in whom some of the spirit that moved Father Junípero evidently still lived.

Along the main road from Palma to Manacor there is a small sign-post pointing in almost indecipherable letters the way to Petra, "birthplace of Fray Junípero Serra". We followed a dusty undulating road across an open countryside, passed through the village of Son Orlandis and came to the long narrow high street of Petra. It smelt powerfully of cow's dung, with which it had been recently and liberally bespattered so that it looked like a particularly long advertisement for a new shade of Waterman's ink. Clearly we were no longer in tourist country, in spite of the little sign-post. Here, it was the native soil that mattered, not the foreign noses, but even so Majorcan passion for cleanliness would tolerate only the freshest unavoidable dung, so that the street did not become a miasma of ageing ordure such as streets in similar towns normally become in other parts of Europe, where they are less nice about these matters.

We drew up in the square opposite a drab cafe from which some rather drab loungers looked at us listlessly. The place wore a distinctly dispirited look, as if Father Junípero, whose statue gazed down upon us, had used up the town's ration of spirit for two hundred years or more. At a bakery we asked where the birthplace was and a young girl volunteered to show us the way. We followed her down quiet symmetrical narrow streets, where no dung was, which crossed each other at right angles, until she stopped at a house indistinguishable from its neighbours. It was a low two-storeyed building, looking with the rough unpainted doors of the livestock room rather like some rustic mews flat. The interior had been fitted up with "period" furniture, including a canopied bed in the nuptial alcove, said to be the precise spot where the Venerable Founder of California entered the world. The garden behind the house had been allowed to run wild and a huge clump of geraniums, gone to seed, filled one corner of it. One can't help feeling that Father Junípero, who was as sensible as he was saintly, would have much preferred that the garden should have been cultivated by some industrious peasant than remain nothing more than a sadly desolate memorial to himself.

As a child Miguel Joseph Ferrer, which was his name before he became a monk, attended the convent of San Bernardino at Petra, and afterwards the Franciscan convent in Palma where he took the cowl towards the end of his sixteenth year. By then he had already become celebrated in Majorca for his piety and scholarship and he was appointed lecturer in philosophy at the Lullian University at Palma. As a preacher he became greatly sought after and his Lenten sermons were events of annual importance in the life of the island.

But the pleasant and peaceful existence of a successful preacher and don did not satisfy Father Serra's thirst for evangelism and in 1748, at the age of thirty-five, he applied to be sent to the Indies with his friend and brother Franciscan, Fray Francisco Palou. Such was the enthusiasm at that time among members of the order to convert the pagan Indians that a year elapsed before the two Majorcans were informed that vacancies were available.

On April 13th, 1749, they set sail for Malaga, ironically enough in an English vessel, whose skipper caused them a good deal of embarrassment. He was, says Palou, "an obstinate heretic and so quarrelsome that during the two weeks the voyage lasted till we reached Malaga, he did not leave us in peace, and it was with difficulty that we could recite the Divine Office, because he continually wished to argue and dispute with us about dogma." In these discussions he was apparently so confounded by Fray Junípero's superior learning, that he threatened to take his own life, which worried the good Fathers so much that they kept watch to prevent him from doing so.

They set sail again from Cadiz in August and after a voyage of ninety-nine days, arrived safely at Vera Cruz with a number of other Majorcan missionaries. Towards the end of the voyage, they had run so short of water that they were not allowed to make chocolate. Fray Junípero's cheerfulness in this distress was as saintly as his remedy for it was practical, namely, "to eat little, to talk less and so save my saliva".

At Vera Cruz, Fray Junípero insisted on performing the last stage of the journey to Mexico City on foot. The distance was nearly three hundred miles and the hardships considerable, but this was only the first of many tremendous journeys on foot which the devoted friar was to make for the rest of his life. During the course of it he contracted an ulcer on his foot, which never completely healed and which must have made a martyrdom of every step of his subsequent journeyings.

At Mexico City, Fray Junípero became a pupil at the Apostolic College of San Fernando of Mexico, but after six months he and his friend Palou were appointed to the missions of the Sierra Gorda in the province of Queretaro, some 130 miles north of Mexico City. He worked in the missions for nine years, during which he achieved considerably success as an evangelist and coloniser. His methods were those which had been tried and found efficacious by the missionaries of other orders in different parts of Spanish America and they were founded on the eminently practical proposition that you must first satisfy a man's belly before you can hope to elevate his spirit. Consequently much of Fray Junípero's time and effort was devoted to the economic welfare of his flock, and for this task the son of a Majorcan husbandman was well fitted. He taught the people how to raise good crops from seeds imported from Spain and with the surplus produce he bought tools and other goods for the community. He encouraged women to work and taught them how to sew and weave. He taught the trades of carpenter and mason, trades which were practised for seven years in the building of a great stone church for the village. It all sounds idyllic and strangely reminiscent of what we are told about communal progress in the villages of certain backward countries today, in which however, the community's store takes the place of the parish church. Of course the progress was compulsory, as it is in Communist China, and any Indian who refused to participate was brought literally into the fold by the simple expedient of burning down his house.

In 1760 Fray Junípero was appointed to a mission to the Apache Indians, but this mission never materialised and that notoriously corybantic tribe were allowed to persist in their primitive exertions, so that more than a century and a half later they were able to divert for a while a connoisseur of such activities, D.H. Lawrence.

For the next seven years Fray Junípero remained attached to the Apostolic College in Mexico City, whence he sallied forth on numerous missionary journeys in the neighbouring country. It was not therefore until he had reached the - for that period - advanced age of fifty-four that he was appointed to take charge of the Franciscan missions in Lower California, an area which had recently been taken over from the Jesuits. Fray Junípero was further charged with one of the last enterprises in the history of Spanish American colonial development, the *Conquista* of Upper California, the area now known simply as California, the thirty-first State of the United States of America.

To this he devoted the remaining seventeen years of his life which, except when he made one more tremendous journey to Mexico City in order to enlist the help of the Viceroy, was entirely spent among the "savage" tribes of Upper California, for savage they seemed to Fray Junípero and his fellow labourers. The men went naked like the Majorcans of old and they were hopelessly polygamous, even to the extent of marrying, not only their wives' sisters, but their mothers-in-law also. Fray Palou reports with wonder the case of one happy family where all the man's wives, consisting of a mother and her daughters, were pregnant at the same time. What happened to the father-in-law is not explained, but presumably he ultimately married HIS mother-in-law. Yet in spite of their outrageous disregard for the table of kindred affinity, the natives appear to have led a happy life and the Franciscan fathers reported that they were very affable. Naked and unashamed - until baptism taught them shame, says Fray Palou triumphantly - though they were, they had apparently succeeded in evolving a way of life, in which sex did not seem to have been the severe problem that more civilised peoples have found it. Even homosexuality was tolerated by the moral or immoral code of this genial people. No wonder that Rousseau and Chateaubriand should have found inspiration in the Happy Savage as contemporary accounts represented him to be!

But all this was soon altered by the saintly Serra and his devoted band of friars. The people were clothed, their wives were rationed and unnatural vice was severely punished. The easy going live and let live philosophy of the pagan countryside was suppressed and superseded by the discipline of a militant Christian settlement. And parallel with this moral discipline went the ordered economy of European civilization. Instead of living from hand to mouth as they had done in the past the natives were instructed how to grow their crops scientifically and how to exploit and develop the fruits which already grew abundantly in their wonderful soil and especially the grape. Fray Junípero showed them how to irrigate their fields and, whenever he founded a new colony, his first consideration was the availability of a good supply of water.

Yet after he had christened and clothed, fed and lodged them, Fray Junípero had no illusions about the spiritual quality of his flock. He was far too sane to expect any great or immediate improvement in this respect. He hoped however, that the example of charity, humility and service set by him and his brothers might make some slight impression. Certainly he did not spare himself in order that this hope should be fulfilled. His endless and agonising journeys on foot and his tireless labours as an evangelist and administrator should have been more than enough to illustrate the quality of service. His charity was displayed even more efficaciously. When one of his brother missionaries was murdered at San Diego, he pleaded with the Viceroy that no reprisals should be taken against the "poor ignorant Indians". The Viceroy granted Fray Junípero's request and the culprits were set at liberty, a piece of magnanimity that can seldom have been paralled in the history of colonial conquest.

In order to impress his flock, the evangelist did not disdain spectacular if painful histrionics. In the pulpit he would chastise himself with the chain he always carried about with him for that purpose. When he had finished his sermons he would lift up the crucifix in his left hand and then take up in his right hand a large stone which he kept concealed in the pulpit and with which he would beat his breast. He also had a large taper with four wicks, which he would light and then apply to his breast, which he would bare for the purpose. All this must have been very startling to the "poor ignorant Indian" with his affable manner and absurdly easy virtue.

While the saintly Majorcan was performing these masochistic exercises to further the Spiritual Conquista and to extend the dominions of His Catholic Majesty, an English Tory of equal piety but less enthusiasm, was telling a friend at dinner in a coffee house that he "loved the University of Salamanca; for when the Spaniards were in doubt as to the lawfulness of their conquering America, the University of Salamanca gave it as their opinion that it was not lawful." Dr Johnson whose hatred of colonies was perhaps exceeded only by his hatred of Whigs and yet who never ceased to preach the principle of subordination, on one occasion "in company with some very grave men of Oxford" drank to "the next insurrection of the negroes in the West Indies". He said on another occasion, "I do not much wish well to discoveries, for I am always afraid they will end in conquest and robbery." When Fray Junípero died a death worthy of his life on St Augustine's Day, 1784, the conquest was virtually complete. The robbery followed in due course and the inhabitants of the settlements of San Diego, Monterey and San Francisco were submerged and virtually extirpated by a more powerful people. If Fray Junípero were able to revisit the cities of his foundation, where his name is now honoured, he would, no doubt, be amazed at their development. He would also deplore the fate of the natives, whose "real culture and progress" he had laboured with so much faith to try and secure. And, if on his return to the Elysian Fields he were to meet his great English contemporary - they died within a few months of each other - it seems unlikely that they would disagree on the subject of the last Conquista in America.

## REVOLUTIONARY

Not many years before Fray Serra founded the city of San Francisco, there was born in Majorca a man who was destined to make a very different contribution to Spanish American history, whose action was in fact to run directly counter to that of his illustrious countryman. Whereas Fray Serra devoted most of his life to the extension both of the Spanish dominions and the Roman Catholic Church, Juan Bautista Picornell y Gomilla dedicated his quixotic genius to the destruction of the first and the enfeeblement of the second.

Yet the ultimate aim of priest and freemason, missionary and revolutionary, seems to have been the same, namely the welfare and progress of the natives of South America. The difference lay in their conception of these desirable objectives and consequently in the methods by which they might hope to be achieved. Fray Serra's ideals depended on a paternalistic and clerical autocracy, Picornell's on a constitutional democracy. The priest looked to the *ancien regime* for the fulfilment of his otherworldly ambitions, the liberal relied upon its destruction for the achievement of his no less lofty aspirations. It was a Majorcan who laid the last brick on the Spanish colonial edifice and it was a Majorcan who struck the first blow at its already crumbling foundations.

Picornell was born at Palma in 1759, the son of a well-to-do landowner; as a youth he must have been influenced by the liberal ideas then about to find expression in the Palma Sociedad Económica. His education was continued at Madrid University where he graduated at the age of twenty. Soon afterwards he married and in 1782 his son Juan Antonio Picornell y Obispo was born. From Madrid Picornell moved to Salamanca where he obtained a post at the Univeristy loved by Johnson and it was there that he caried out on his infant son his celebrated experiment in primary education.

Picornell believed that the capacity to learn was greatest in extreme youth and that, provided the correct methods were used, a child, irrespective of his intelligence and whether or not he knew his letters, could be taught infinitely more than was traditionally considered possible. To prove his theories he submitted baby Picornell to a public examination in fourteen subjects ranging from "Dogma, mysteries and elements of religion and morals" to "First inhabitants of the Peninsula; origin and etymology of their name". The child passed the test triumphantly and the proud father published his first work entitled 'A Public Examination, Catechistic, Historical and Geographical to which Don Juan Picornell y Gomilla, Fellow of the Royal Economic Society of Madrid, submitted his son Juan Antonio Picornell y Obispo aged three years six months and twenty four days at the University of Salamanca on Sunday 3 April this year (1785) at ten o'clock in the Morning."

Encouraged by the success of his early essays in progressive education and enjoying the protection of the Spanish Prime Minister Florida Blanca, Picornell sought to have his ideas put into practice, but they were too advanced for the Spanish official mind, which saw in the reforms proposed by Picornell serious dangers for the established order of things. Disillusioned and disgusted by the cynical manner in which his proposals were rejected and encouraged no doubt by the events on the other side of the Pyrenees - the year was 1790 - the young Majorcan professor turned revolutionary. He also became a freemason and was initiated into the lodge recently founded in Spain by Count Cagliostro. From then onwards and with little intermission for the rest of his life he dedicated himself to the propagation of the principles summarised the previous year in "The Declaration of the Rights of Man". At the beginning of 1793 he was given an admirable opportunity for this task when he was sent by Florida Blanca on a tour of the Spanish provinces to investigate the state of their economy, rather as Arthur Young had been doing in France some years before and as Cobbett was to do later in England.

On his return to Madrid, Picornell began to plan actively the overthrow of the monarchy and its substitution by a republic on the French pattern. During the whole of 1794 he worked incessantly recruiting supporters and collecting arms and towards the end of the year he left his wife and adored only son to devote himself exclusively to the final preparations for the revolution and to compose two pamphlets, his "Manifesto" and his "Instruction". The first was designed to explain to the people why it was necessary to destroy the existing regime and the second contained detailed instructions on the conduct of the rebellion. February 3, the festival of San Blas was fixed for the outbreak but in the early hours of that morning Picornell and the other ringleaders were arrested and the conspiracy collapsed. It had been betrayed at the last moment by a faint-heart.

After a trial lasting more than a year and after enduring tortures that totally failed to break their spirit, Picornell and his four principal associates were condemned to death. But thanks to the pleading of a distinguished lawyer Don Francisco Perez de Lerma, whom the King, Charles IV, had directed to review the conduct of the trial, the sentence was commuted to one of life imprisonment in the gaols of the New World.

Picornell's wife and son, neither of whom he was to see again and whom he had kept in ignorance of his revolutionary activities, were both imprisoned. Although he was only thirteen when the plot was discovered, Juan Antonio was not released until two and a half years later, when he was permitted to retire with his mother to Majorca to be in the charge of his uncle, Lucas Picornell. The boy must have been a headache to Uncle Lucas, for undaunted by his father's fate and inspired by his example and teaching, he at once joined the liberals in their battle with the clerical party. The young prodigy from Salamanca proved a most effective reinforcement and confounded his opponents with the brilliance and force of his polemics. He later turned his attention to the stuffy "Diario de Mallorca", the island's first daily paper, and subjected it to such drastic criticism in a series of Letters that the Editor to whom they were addressed resigned his office to his formidable correspondent.

With the outbreak of the Peninsular War and the temporary eclipse of the liberal party in Majorca, Picornell junior was advised to leave the island in case the authorities should take action against him. He took the advice and in 1805 set off for the New World, in a vain search for his father, who was then in Europe. The son's fruitless quest ended nine years later when he died somewhere in Mexico.

Like Fray Serra nearly fifty years earlier Picornell was provided by the Spanish Government with a free passage to the Indies. He set sail from Corunna on 24 October 1796 in the barquentine "La Golondrina" and arrived at La Guaira sixteen weeks later after a voyage compared with which Fray Serra's must have been a pleasure cruise. If the missionary suffered all his life from self-inflicted wounds, the revolutionary convict carried with him to the grave the marks left by the unspeakably heavy irons in which his wrists and ankles festered for nearly two years.

At La Guaira, the chief port of what is now Venezuela, Picornell found himself among friends and sympathisers. A fellow Majorcan sent him *ensaimadas* (Majorcan sugar buns), the Governor of the gaol, at Picornell's suggestion, engaged him to give lessons to his children, the Sergeant of the guard and the prison doctors acted as channels of communication with the outside world and the barber of La Guaira, true to the tradition set by his more famous colleague of Seville, used his shop as a clearing house for Picornell's propaganda. For within a few weeks of his arrival in the New World the Majorcan was busy spreading the gospel, not indeed of the Catholic Church but of Rousseau and Voltaire. His slogan was not "Serve God, Honour the King" but "Liberté, Egalité, Fraternité". Almost everyone who came in contact with him fell under the spell of his persuasive genius and the political and moral treatises, fables, satires, manifestos and patriotic songs, that he composed in his cell were copied and re-copied by their enthusiastic readers until they were disseminated all over the Captain Generalcy of Caracas and beyond.

From propaganda in order to convert, Picornell and his adherents passed once more to action to overthrow the established order. Still from the confinement of his cell, he drew up a plan of rebellion which was carried out under the direction of two leading residents of La Guaira, Gual and España, after whom the conspiracy is now generally named.

As a useful preliminary to their operations the conspirators decided that Picornell should be rescued from prison. Their first scheme, which involved the use of a rope, was abortive and the prisoner was finally released by the head gaoler, who had joined the revolutionary party. After some weeks hiding in the countryside between La Guaira and Caracas, the hue and cry became so intense that the fugitive was in danger of being recaptured. He was therefore put on a small boat which landed him on the island of Curacao, whence he sailed immediately for Guadeloupe.

The conspiracy of Gual and España, like that of San Blas, was betrayed soon afterwards and those of its leaders who escaped arrest, took refuge with Picornell in the French and British West Indian colonies and from them continued their revolutionary activities. In Guadeloupe, Picornell busied himself with propaganda and produced his Spanish translation of the "Rights of Man together with Various Republican Maxims and a Preliminary Discourse Directed to Americans". This work and a translation of the French revolutionary song "La Carmagnole" were printed by Picornell and distributed to prepare the ground for further attempts to overthrow the colonial regime in Caracas.

With the conclusion of peace between France and Spain by the Treaty of Basle the revolutionaries could expect to receive no further support from the French republican governor of Guadeloupe and they therefore turned to the English, who were still at war with Spain. In Trinidad recently captured from the Spaniards, Picornell received a warm welcome from its first and well-loved British governor, Thomas Picton, better known to posterity as the eccentric hero killed at Waterloo. Picton was full of ideas how the mainland could be freed from the monopolistic and despotic rule of Spain and in May 1798 he suggested to the C. in C. West Indies that a force should be sent in the autumn of that year to assist the citizens of Cumana to rid themselves of their colonial oppressors. He added that "I have a person perfectly master of the Spanish language who can prepare all the necessary declarations and papers." This person sounds suspiciously like Picornell.

For two years the Majorcan revolutionary lived on the charity of the British soldier, hoping to receive for his schemes that material aid which, with the peace preliminaries between England and Spain, became steadily more remote. Thomas Picton and Juan Bautista Picornell, the man of action and the philosopher, the warrior and the pacifist, the stern administrator and the benevolent rebel, the Welsh country gentleman and the Majorcan intellectual; one cannot help wondering how two such different characters got on with each other. At least they had one thing in common; they both had a price on their head, a high price offered by a nervous and decrepit Captain General in Caracas. The reactions of the two intended victims are curious to compare. Picornell, the man of peace, sought out his would-be assassins sword in hand, while Picton the man of war sent the Captain General the following letter:

Trinidad 25th January 1799

Sir

Your excellency has highly flattered my vanity by the very handsome value which you have been pleased to fix upon my head. Twenty thousand dollars is an offer which would not discredit your royal master's munificence!

As the trifle has had the good fortune to recommend itself to your excellency's attention, come and take it and it will be much at your service: in expectation of which I have the honour to be etc. etc.

Thomas Picton

His excellency, Don Pedro Carbonelli [*sic*]

Governor General, Caraccas [*sic*]

The negotiations preceding the Peace of Amiens finally ruled out any possibility of a joint operation by Picton and the rebels and in 1800 Picornell decided to leave Trinidad for London. Falling ill at Barbados, he felt unable to continue the voyage and instead sailed north to Philadelphia, whose free fresh air he breathed for the next five years under an assumed name. It was shortly before Trafalgar that he eventually crossed the Atlantic for the second time and for some years he seems to have practised as a doctor in Paris to whose medical faculty he was admitted.

In 1810 another revolution which broke out in Venezuela was successful. Doctor Picornell gave up his practice and travelling via London offered his services to the rebel leaders, Miranda and Bolivar. He was coldly received and instead of being given the portfolio of education, as he had hoped, he was fobbed off with the post of Chief of Police at Caracas, an uncomfortable situation, one imagines, for a subversive person. He did not have to endure it for long and within a few months of his return to Venezuela he was obliged to flee the country once again before a victorious Spanish army.

The knight errant of the Rights of Man went back to Philadelphia where he was soon engaged in a fresh revolutionary scheme this time for invading Mexico. He was appointed secretary to the rebel leadership and entrusted with propaganda and the editing of a newspaper called the "Texas Gazette". The appointment was not a success and, tiring of the constant bickering between the leaders he moved on to New Orleans, where yet another expedition to liberate Mexico was being organised. Picornell was elected President of the future Republic, in which exalted position he had the pleasant task of appealing to his former superiors to rally round himself. The appeal was indignantly ignored.

It was at this point that Picornell took a surprising decision. At the very moment when, as a result of his eloquent propaganda, support for the enterprise was beginning to roll in, the President-elect abandoned it and through the agency of a Capuchin friar sought and eventually obtained the Royal Pardon for all his crimes against the Spanish state. The Majorcan's apologists argue convincingly that this curious action was not a betrayal of his principles but a calculated step to enable him, not only to disassociate himself from a gang of self-seeking filibusters, but to work more effectively for the promotion of the republican cause. Certainly the Spanish authorities in America did not believe that he had seriously renounced his political faith nor that he would miss any opportunity of spreading it. It is significant too that his pardon was obtained through the medium of a member of an order, which Picton had regarded as thoroughly disaffected with Spanish colonial rule.

If Picornell had been guilty of a betrayal he did not seek to profit materially by it nor did he return to Spain to claim the pensions and places that had been promised him. He did however take advantage of the Royal pardon to apply for the post of secretary to the Spanish consul at New Orleans, where he would be well placed to carry on his subversive activities. His application was more successful than he had perhaps anticipated. Not only did he obtain the job, but the consul, who soon succumbed to the Majorcan's teachings, collaborated with him in a new scheme he was preparing to liberate Cuba.

In June 1819 a serious epidemic of Yellow Fever in New Orleans diverted Picornell once more from politics to medicine. The local authorities needed a medical man, who spoke French, Spanish and English, to take charge of the quarantine station established as a result of the epidemic. Picornell had the required qualifications and was appointed the first director. He had then spent sixty years of an exhausting and dangerous life and he could scarcely have been blamed if he had treated this new official appointment as something of a sinecure. Instead he took advantage of the facilities it afforded to explore the "medical topography" of New Orleans.

He was horrified by what he found, and since his reforming zeal was still unquenched, set about the task of showing the citizens of New Orleans what squalor they lived in and what steps they should take to remedy it. His last essay in public enlightenment entitled "Considerations hygieniques sur la Nouvelle Orleans", was published in 1823 by a French doctor to whom he had given the manuscript. The "Considerations" reveal as much as anything he ever wrote, this Majorcan's humanity and good sense as well as his ability to popularise the unlikeliest subjects. In order, for example, to convey to the general reader the harmful effects of insufficient ventilation he describes a prison, readily identifiable by any English schoolboy as the Black Hole. To ensure that the muzziest alderman should catch the point, he goes on to relate how in 1559 all those present at a trial in Oxford died of asphyxiation in an airless courtroom, an episode that has received less publicity than the more recent tragedy at Calcutta, the Black Hole.

It might have been expected that Picornell would have spent his declining years in a city where he was not without honour, busying himself with a General Pharmacopoeia for use throughout the United States, with whose preparation he had been entrusted. But the Pharmacopoeia was never completed and perhaps was never begun and the ageing doctor, for reasons that are unknown - did he want to get out of this new undertaking? - departed from New Orleans and sometime in 1820 set up in medical practice in Cuba in the small town of Puerto Principe. It is possible that his decision to go to Cuba may have been connected with his schemes for its liberation but whatever the reason, he did not benefit financially by the move and died in poverty and obscurity five years later at the age of sixty-six.

## AFRANCESADO

Spanish historians divide Spaniards in the XVIIIth century into three main political categories, the absolutists of whom Fray Serra may be regarded as a fair representative, the liberals to whom Picornell belongs and the "Afrancesados" among whom Cristobal Cladera occupies a distinguished place. To attempt to define fully the term "Afrancesado" would be beyond the scope of this book, but roughly speaking, it meant a person who believed in the political, social and economic teachings of the French encyclopaedists to the extent that they were compatible with a monarchical form of government. They were not republicans but advocates of enlightened autocracy whose model was Prussia under that much admired *afrancesado*, Frederick the Great. The Bourbon King of Spain, Charles III went some way to fulfilling their ideals, but the reign of his successor, Charles IV, was a reversion to and an exaggeration of obscurantist absolutism. When therefore a summary end was put to it by Napoleon, the *afrancesados* were ready to welcome the usurpation of the throne of Spain by his brother, Joseph, as the beginning of a new era of enlightenment. Those of them who like Cladera came from Majorca, may also have felt that the House of Bonaparte, which had long been settled in that island before it moved to Corsica, might provide a monarch for Spain with more propriety than either the Austrian Hapsburgs or the French Bourbons.

It is as a prominent *afrancesado* that Cladera is still mentioned in Majorcan and Spanish history, but my interest in him was aroused by another and less controversial aspect of his career. It happened in this way. While turning over the pages of the programme given me by Madalena's aunt, herself incidentally a member of the Cladera family, my eye caught the word "Hamlet". Shakespeare in La Puebla surprised me as much as a street called "Greene" and I read what would otherwise in all probability have remained unread, and discovered a Majorcan student of English literature, long since forgotten, but who deserves to be recalled.

Cristobal Cladera was born at La Puebla on 10th December, 1760 into a family that had been established in Majorca since its conquest by Aragon. From the tenderest age, we are told, he showed a marked taste for literature and it is hardly surprising that, as a student he should not have been content with the intellectual fare provided by the University of Palma, which seems to have been scarcely more invigorating than what was offered by the University of Oxford to Edward Gibbon a generation earlier. "More than prosaic, pedestrian is the epithet that should be applied to that culture of tasteless savants, of grandiloquent sophists, of baroque poet-tasters, of sycophantic placemen and long-winded friars" says the Majorcan historian, Oliver of Majorcan culture in the last half of the XVIIIth century.

Nevertheless, efforts were being made by the Sociedad de los Amigos del Pais to stimulate interest in the literature of other countries, particularly France and England. Thanks to their propaganda "Robinson Crusoe" became one of the most popular books in the island while the novels of Richardson and Fielding and even the poetry of Milton and Pope were read by a select few. It is quite probable therefore, that Cladera owed his taste for the English language and literature, which later characterised him, to some extent to that small group of cultivated Majorcans, then busily engaged in letting fresh European air into many a rancid Palma *tertulia*.

From Palma, Cladera went to various Universities in Spain of which the last was Valencia, where he took his doctorate in law. Having also taken Holy Orders, he was given a chaplaincy at the Cathedral of Seville and shortly afterwards in May 1782, he was appointed Treasurer of Palma Cathedral. This office seems to have been something of a sinecure, for having taken formal possession of it, Cladera removed himself almost at once to Madrid, where he soon acquired another "place". A Majorcan, named Bernardo Nadal, having been elected Bishop of Palma, the Treasurer stepped into his shoes as head of the Secretariat for the Interpretation of Languages.

Even if he was a placeman and a pluralist, he was not idle and during these Madrid years Cladera published a large number of works, including his "Espiritu de Los Mejores Diarios que se Publican en Europa", a precursor of the "Reader's Digest" of our own times. Cladera's "Works" do not make light reading and Señor Oliver would no doubt classify him as a "sycophantic placeman" and a "long-winded friar". In one of his books, on the subject of Captain Cook's Voyages, there is an interminable dedication to Godoy, in which the Prince of the Peace's ancestry is traced back to the Cid and written in language of such outrageous adulation that one wonders whether, after all, the author of it is not best forgotten. But flattery of a distinguished patron was not considered any more ignoble in those days than flattery of the public is now, and if Cladera was guilty of a a servile dedication, he also had the merit later of suffering exile and ruin for the sake of his opinions.

During his period of prosperity he was able to travel extensively abroad and one of his journeys took him to England where, according to his Majorcan biographer, he was received with applause and acclamation and where his talents and virtues were widely recognised. I have not been able to discover any details of this visit to England and it is quite possible that the *éclat* with which it is alleged to have been attended, may have been exaggerated. However, it is more than likely that a distinguished Spanish divine of liberal views, the author of "Reflections on Religious Intolerance", the translator of Edward Young's "The Last Day" and of Addison's "Reflections", which I have not succeeded in identifying, and the author of an "Examination of the tragedy entitled Hamlet written in English by Guillermo Shakespeare, translated into Castilian by Inarc Arcade"* would have received a polite welcome in English literary and blue-stocking circles.

The events of 1808, not least the massacre of the Dos de Mayo, put an end to Cladera's career and execration instead of applause was reserved for his last years. Appointed to represent Majorca in the so-called Cortes summoned by Napoleon at Bayonne in June 1808, Cladera was at once branded as a leading member of that detested but ill-understood and falsely represented party of "afrancesados". It was inevitable however that they should have been detested, by the Church and the absolutists for collaborating with the representatives of a militantly secular regime, by the liberals for collaborating with a menace to Spain's national independence and by the people for collaborating with a plundering army. In no part of Spain at that time was the Church so influential as it was in Majorca, and Cladera, as a dignitary of that Church

---

* Arcade was presumably the pseudonym used by Moratin, whose translation of "Hamlet", the first in the Spanish language, appeared in 1798, five years after his visit to England, in order to prepare himself for the work. It was this translation that incurred Cladera's censure, which, however, Moratin ignored.

was regarded as an apostate as well as a traitor. Action was taken against him and the revenues belonging to the office of Treasurer of the Cathedral were confiscated by the Junta, who needed every duro they could lay their hands on, owing to the unprecedented demands made on the island's financial resources by the wartime emergency.

Cladera was not to be intimidated by the fury of his fellow islanders and in 1813, having prudently retreated with King Joseph from Spain into France, he instituted proceedings at the Ecclesiastical Tribunal of Majorca in order to recover his lost rights. The following year this bold, if not impudent, action was rewarded and when peace was restored he obtained permission from Ferdinand VII to return to Majorca to prosecute his suit on the spot. He seems to have done so successfully but he did not live long to enjoy the fruits of a Treasuryship regained. He died on the 19th December, 1816 at his country house of Son Fe, near Alcudia, whither he had retired after his return to Majorca.

I was curious to visit the house which had seen the last years of the author of an "Examination of the tragedy entitled Hamlet" but it was not until the very last day of our stay that we succeeded in locating it. We found it just off the main Alcudia/Palma road, not very far from that other place with its English associations, the ruined village of Gata Moix. The house is built on the slope of a hill and the lower side of the site is shored up, as it were, by a massive stone wall which we drove past at first, thinking the house must be further on. It was to all intents and purposes an ordinary Majorcan farm house, that is to say, a small stone square dwelling for the farmer and his family with the stable and cowshed adjoining it and in this case, filling the space between the dwelling and the terrace wall. There was yet something about the buildings that suggested they had once been more than they obviously are now and encouraged us to think that we were indeed visiting the rural retreat of Cristobal Cladera.

The farmer, a cheerful ruddy-faced middle-aged man, had never heard of him, but perhaps his father had? This ancient person, with his equally ancient wife, was sitting under a kind of penthouse, rocking himself gently in a very low chair. He was well over eighty he said and had lived at Son Fe all his life. He thought he had heard of Cladera, but couldn't be sure. It was indeed likely enough that he had lived at Son Fe, as the property had once belonged to the Church, and that was as much as he would say about it.

The son invited us into the house and showed us the gothic arches clearly outlined in the plaster walls in which some improving lay landlord had embedded them. Outside, there were other traces of Son Fe's better days and ecclesiastical origins. In the farmyard wall were the vestiges of a large and handsome sun dial. Near the penthouse, where the old man was still gently rocking himself, were a few dressed stones, all that remained of the chapel that once stood there. Over the entrance to the farmyard there had formerly been an archway and some of the stones belonging to it still served to support the farmer's gate. The end stones of the great terrace wall were moulded, showing that utility had not been the sole consideration in its construction and that the place must once have been something more than a simple farm-house.

The farmer, though he was not in the least interested in the purpose of our visit, made us very welcome and after we had seen all the stones he could show us, sat us down in the parlour, each to a glass of water freshly drawn from the spring of Son Fe, well-known in the neighbourhood he assured us, for its excellence. We expressed our appreciation, listened to his stolid account of the accidental death of his only son, admired the photograph of his daughter and her military husband and then, since it was our last day, took our leave; passed under the vine trellis, nodded to the rocking man and drove away through the fertile fields, thinking perhaps that it was not a bad place even now for a Treasurer and "afrancesado" or even a humble farmer's father to die at.

## LIBERAL

Most Majorcans, however long they may stay abroad in search of fame and fortune, like to spend their declining years in the peaceful shelter of their native island. It must therefore be a great sadness to any of them to whom this consolation is denied and doubly sad when, as was the fate of Cladera's great contemporary, Felipe Bauza, the evil days had to be faced alone in a London slum.

Bauza was born in 1764 in the village of Deyá, which is described, conceivably by himself in Alexander Laborde's "Voyage Pittoresque D'Espagne" as "built on an eminence and the spiritual jurisdiction belongs to the parish of Valldemosa, from which it was separated as to its temporal government in the year 1550; it has a church and a vicar, a bailiff and a Christian school." Like his father, young Felipe went into the Spanish navy, in which he had an honourable and active career. Soon after joining he took part in the recapture of Minorca from the British in 1782 and this must have been the first occasion on which he met or had any dealings with members of a nation, with which much of his later life was to be intimately associated.

Very early in his career Bauza devoted himself to his principal and abiding interest, which was maps and map making. In this he showed himself to be a worthy inheritor of a great Majorcan tradition, for the maps of the Palma cartographers were once the wonder and the envy of the world, while the discovery of the magnetic compass has also been claimed for Majorca. In the 14th century, when Palma was the principal entrepôt in the Western Mediterranean for trade between the West and the East, her maps were so excellent that the Italian map makers were in the habit of attributing their own maps to Majorcan geographers. Jafuda Cresques, known as "the Compass Jew", who lived in Majorca from 1381 to 1394, was responsible for the famous Mapa Mundi which John I of Aragon gave to Charles VI of France and which is now in the Louvre. Cresques later became Director of the Maritime School established at Sagres in Portugal. Majorcan maps continued, until the seventeenth century, to be sought after by foreign navigators chiefly Italians, but not perhaps Christopher Columbus who, according to two books published in 1990 *La Verdad de Juan Colom* and *El Descubridor del Nuevo Mundo*, was a Majorcan. The author, Jaume Amengual, embarked on years of research after being told by Rafael Bauza that he, through his mother, was the sole descendant of Columbus. According to family tradition, he was born at Andraitx and married to a native of Montuïri. From her he had learnt of the existence of the New World, which the mapmakers of Montuïri had for generations kept secret. Examples of Majorcan maps are now to be found in the libraries of Bologna, Venice and Rome and also in Paris and at the British Museum.

One of the few early Majorcan maps to be seen now in Majorca is the one that was involved in the accident described by George Sand in "Un Hiver a Majorque". It is a map of the Azores, made by Vallseca in 1439 and was brought back from Italy by Cardinal Despuig, in whose country mansion of Raxa George Sand was shown it. According to her account, it was the foolish servant who used a bottle of ink as a paper weight which, not being heavy enough, was upset by the stiff parchment rolling up into its customary cylindrical state. Then did the Black Sea become literally black, joked La Sand, a little unseasonably perhaps. The Majorcans were not amused and one of the island's learned historians has asserted that it was not the servant but Madame Sand herself, who spilt the ink, either deliberately out of malice, or by accident.

In 1785 Bauza was engaged in preparing the Maritime Atlas of Spain and some years later he was sent to South America to carry out a number of surveys including one in 1794 of the country between Buenos Aires and Santiago de Chile, Of his work at that time, it is recorded in the Proceedings of the Royal Geographical Society that "the methods and instruments used by Bauza were not adopted, if known, by French or English surveyors until afterwards" and "the most perfect style of plan drawing on true principals etc. were practised by Spaniards before this century (the 19th) commenced." Alexander von Humboldt, who was perhaps better fitted than anyone to estimate the value of Bauza's contribution to the cartography of South America, refers to him as "the eminent geographer". He mentions also Bauza's collaboration with that passionate liberal Isidoro de Antillon, who should be the patron saint of Spanish schoolboys, since it was he who abolished beating in Spanish schools. Antillon, who is celebrated in the annals of Majorca as the representative at Palma of the Central Junta of Cadiz and as the founder of the Majorcan liberal newspaper "Aurora", considered that Bauza was not only an honour to Majorca, but the "great man of Europe".

In 1796, when he was serving in a frigate named - ironically so far as he was concerned - the *Mahonesa*, Bauza was taken prisoner by H.M.S. *Terpsichore* and he was thus able to renew his acquaintance with the English, begun fourteen years previously when he had been the captor of some of them at Port Mahon. After his release he was appointed Chief Hydrographer at Madrid, a position which he held in 1804, when he was a frequent guest at dinner parties given by Lord and Lady Holland. In 1808 he succeeded in escaping from the French invaders and Lady Holland, who was again in Spain, and who probably met him at Seville, noted in her diary, "Bauza with great dexterity has contrived to make his escape from Madrid with his family and all his most valuable papers, and to conceal the rest so that the French can have no access to them - his materials for a map of the provinces of Spain bordering on the Pyrenees, Malespina's voyage, the drawings and various materials for South America etc. Laborde, who had been employed on the "Voyage Pittoresque D'Espagne"* persecuted him. The French officers are very corrupt and money will procure any testimony. For five guineas he got a certificate from a mulatto colonel to declare he was 60 years of age. He describes the people of Madrid etc."

From 1808 until 1812 Bauza carried out important tasks on behalf both of

*An English translation of this monumental work appeared in 1809. In the advertisement the English Editor writes, "In the translation few liberties have been taken with the original text: some compliments to the reigning family of France, and particularly to Joseph Buonaparte, in our author's estimation the destined, if not the reigning, monarch of Spain, have been omitted, as too fulsome for an English ear." In view of the popular detestation in which Boney and the French were held at that time, this prefatory understatement is a nice indication of the extent to which it was then possible to remain aloof from the passions of the populace.

the Central Junta and General Graham, then commanding the British troops at Cadiz and the Isla de Leon. One of the people with whom he had to work was Graham's chief of staff, Colonel Cathcart. Years later, during the course of one of his many visits to Spain, Graham, who had by then become Lord Lynedoch, met Bauza by chance at Tolosa and wrote off at once to Cathcart: "I was surprised two hours ago by a visit from your Cadiz friend, Mr. B. (I forget his name already), whom you had such intimacy with about the topography of the country towards Tarifa. He is now employed as chief to have a new map of Spain made by the best people he can find in the different parts of the country. He inquired much after you."

The Second Earl Cathcart was the author of, amongst other works, a paper "On the Phenomenon in the neighbourhood of Edinburgh of the igneous Rocks in their relations to the Secondary Strata". No doubt he and Bauza had much in common.

When it became evident in 1812 that the French would be driven out of Madrid, the devoted Bauza, being anxious for the safety of the documents he had concealed, went on ahead of the advancing Allied armies and was able to rescue not only the papers belonging to the Depósito Hidrográfico but also a large part of the archives of other Ministries before they could be destroyed in the general pillage that accompanied the French withdrawal.

During the next ten years Bauza seems to have been quietly employed with the work of mapping the northern provinces of Spain, but in 1822 he was elected to the Cortes as deputy for Majorca. This was at once the cause of his material ruin and the chief reason why he is still remembered. As a colleague of the martyred Antillon, a friend of the Hollands and a man of science, Bauza could scarcely have been other than a liberal in politics. Inevitably therefore, he joined the ranks of those Spanish statesmen, who sought to put an end to the intolerable and grotesque tyranny of Ferdinand VII. On the 11th January 1823 the Cortes, meeting at Cadiz, voted that the King should be deposed and replaced by a Council of Regency. This attempt to overthrow the regime failed and Bauza and all the deputies who had taken part in it, were condemned to death by garrotting and their possessions were forfeited to the State.

Bauza succeeded in escaping to Gibraltar and from there to London, which was to be his home until his death eleven years later. Thus it was that, in the words of his Majorcan biographer, "when Spain did not know how to pardon her greatest son, he found in the capital of England the due reward of his outstanding merit and a wide appreciation of his talents." Señor Bover has perhaps overstated the case a little in referring to Bauza as Spain's "greatest son", and it is doubtful if the exiled geographer received quite as much recognition as he makes out. Nevertheless he was provided by the British Government with the means to enable him to continue his life's work. This included further journeys to South America and the ascent of the great volcano, Chimborazo.

During the year immediately preceding his exile, Bauza made the acquaintance of a most remarkable personage, who happened to be travelling in Spain at that time. This was "Colonel" or "Count" Francis Maceroni, that 19th century Munchhausen, soldier of fortune, inventor of genius, radical Jack and earliest of frogmen. When he was in Spain, Maceroni obtained from Bauza a map of Nicaragua, that had probably been made by Bauza himself. The inventor had been closely investigating "the subject of a ship communication between the Atlantic and Pacific Oceans" and "having also consulted Baron Humboldt" was "convinced of its practicability by means of the river St. Juan and the lake of Nicaragua." On his return to England, which coincided almost exactly with Bauza's flight, Maceroni succeeded in forming a company with the object of "establishing a ship navigation through a part of Central America, which affords the greatest facilities for such an undertaking." One of the directors was Sir William Congreve, the inventor of the "Congreve" rocket, but the principal director was Felipe Bauza. In the prospectus issued by Maceroni it was stated that a survey obtained from the Hydrographical Cabinet of the Spanish Minister of Marine, which contained "a correct description of the situation most favourable to the undertaking" was in possession of the Company. This was evidently the map Maceroni had obtained from Bauza and for which he received £2,000 and 200 shares. But the great scheme came to nothing and the Company collapsed in the financial panic of 1825. Maceroni later succeeded in selling the idea, presumably with the help of Bauza's £2,000 map to the King of Holland, but though some Dutch surveyors were sent to Nicaragua, nothing further was done about it.

The Spanish Government, no doubt feeling his loss, repeatedly urged Bauza to return to Spain, but he thought it unwise to trust their assurances that no reprisals would be taken against him. Only when a general amnesty of all political offenders was proclaimed by the liberal government of Queen Cristina, did Bauza decide to return to his native country and his family, but then it was too late.

The house No. 52 Johnson Street (now Cranleigh Street), in which Bauza spent his last years and suffered the apoplectic stroke which carried him off, was still to be seen in 1955 by anyone who was curious and cared to explore the immediate environs of Euston Station. It is a depressing neighbourhood even now, but what Somers Town must have been like on March 11th, 1834, when Bauza breathed his last, can scarcely be imagined. More than a century has gone by since that day and what was the most insanitary corner of what was once among the most insanitary cities in the world has been replaced by a modern housing estate. Built about 1770 by one Jacob Leroux, on land belonging to Lord Somers, the district became the resort of refugees from the French Revolution and after them of other impoverished exiles, some of whom, like Bauza, had been largely responsible for the restoration to their country and properties of their French predecessors.

Many of the unfortunate refugees who did not live to see again their native land, were buried in Old St Pancras Church, but Bauza was not among them. According to his Majorcan biographer, whose claims for his distinguished countryman verge sometimes on the grandiloquent, he was buried in Westminster Abbey, but this is not so and I have not been able to discover his grave. Nor, as the same biographer alleges, was he made a Knight of the Garter, but he was an Honorary F.R.G.S., in fact one of the earliest and one cannot help wondering if Señor Bover may not have got a little muddled and thought that the initials stood for Fellow of the "Royal Garter Society". He had also been an Honorary Fellow of the Royal Society since 1819, but in spite of this and a number of foreign academic and scientific distinctions, his death was unnoticed, with one exception, by the entire British press, too busily reporting rapes and murders and the humanity of a Countess in taking to hospital a man run over by her carriage. The exception was the radical

"Times", which printed, as it rarely did at that time, a long and generous obituary of the distinguished exile.

In spite of the indifference of the press Bauza's name did not immediately pass into complete oblivion, and nineteen years after his death, when the possibilities of a canal to link the Atlantic with the Pacific, this time across the isthmus of Panama were being discussed by the Royal Geographical Society, Captain Robert Fitzroy R.N. who read a paper to the Fellows on the subject, stated that "Humboldt had a plan of Cupica* by the well-known Bauza and we now have that made recently by order of the Admiralty." It seems appropriate that the memory of this devoted and enlightened geographer should have been preserved for even so short a period by his association, slight though it was, with one of the most important developments in the progress of the New World.

*This was being considered as one of the possible Pacific entrances of the proposed canal.

# CHAPTER VI
## MAJORCA AT WAR

The first English traveller to publish an account of a visit to Majorca was Sir John Carr, from whose "Travels in Spain and the Balearics", I have already several times quoted. This work appeared in 1811 and was dedicated to Lord Holland, most distinguished of contemporary Hispanophiles. The author who in the preface gives his address as 2 Garden Court, Temple and describes himself on the title page as a K.C. and a member of the Middle Temple, seems to have been neither if the Society's records are to be relied upon. He was however indubitably knighted in 1805 by the Duke of Bedford, when Lord Lieutenant of Ireland, though how he earned the honour is also something of a mystery. Perhaps it was a reward for one of his many "Tours" entitled "A Stranger in Ireland".

The earliest of these "Tours" was a journey from Sir John's birthplace Totnes in Devon to Paris in 1802. There followed a number of similar "Tours" in various parts of Europe and the United Kingdom, which were offered to the public with such regularity that they evidently became rather a joke in some circles and finally provoked a parody called "My Pocket Book". This so enraged the knight that he took proceedings against the publishers, claiming that his literary reputation had been so injured that he had been unable to sell a MS of yet another "Tour", this time in Scotland. The case was heard by Lord Ellenborough, who in an historic judgment held that literary criticism was allowable however severe, if it was not personally libellous against the author. Sir John, though he lost his case, was not discouraged and departed the following year on his "Descriptive Travels in the Southern and Eastern Parts of Spain and the Balearic Islands".

Almost everybody who was anybody was in Spain that year, the year of Corunna, either in the army or in its way. The Hollands were progressing officiously from Seville to Cadiz and from Cadiz to Seville, sampling Tio Pepe's ancestors at Mr Gordon's hospitable table and themselves entertaining at dinner all and sundry, including Jovellanos, Frederick North and a Colonel Whittingham, later to become celebrated in the very un-military history of Majorca. The Hollands had already left for England when Byron arrived at Cadiz, but Sir John Carr was there to meet him. Byron wrote home "I have seen Sir John Carr at Seville and Cadiz and like Swift's barber, have been down on my knees to beg he would not put me into black and white." The tourist took the peer at his word and there is not even so much as a veiled reference to the poet in the "Descriptive Travels". Byron, no doubt offended, retaliated by devoting three stanzas in "Childe Harold" to Carr, which were however subsequently suppressed:

Ye, who would more of Spain and Spaniards know
Sights, saints, antiques, arts, anecdotes and war,
Go hie ye hence to Paternoster Row.
Are they not written in the boke of Carr?
Green Erin's Knight and Europe's star.
Then listen readers to the Man of Ink
Hear what he did and sought and wrote afar
All these are coop'd within one Quarto's brink
This borrow, steal (don't buy) and tell me what you think.

This is pretty cheap doggerel, which even Byron, never hypercritical of his own work, evidently thought or was persuaded by his friends to think unfit to be "put into black and white".

Though one would not think it from reading his book, Carr visited Majorca at one of the most important moments in her modern history, when as a result of events in Spain and Europe, her internal affairs were undergoing drastic changes, while internationally she was again becoming a subject of interest.

Majorca was as eager in the movement of resistance to the French as any part of Spain and on May 29th, 1808, a Supreme Junta was set up at Palma to carry on the government on behalf of the exiled King Ferdinand. One of the first acts of the Junta was to set free a number of English prisoners of war* and hand them over to the British Vice-Consul, and the day after its constitution, a Swiss colonel was despatched with a letter from the Captain General to the commander of the British frigate "Cyane", then cruising off Majorca. The letter stated that as the people of Majorca had no intention of submitting to the usurpation of Napoleon's brother King Joseph, the Supreme Junta wished to discuss measures by which the interests of the lawful King of Spain and his British allies could best be served. Captain Staines took the letter at once to Vice-Admiral Sir Edward Thornbrough, who in turn forwarded it to a harrassed and ailing Commander-in-Chief, Lord Collingwood, who had just ceased his long and devoted vigil outside Toulon. He was now chiefly concerned, in the instructions he sent in reply to his Second in Command, to preserve the Balearic Islands at all costs from the French. He therefore directed Admiral Thornbrough to offer a convention to the Captain General, which would provide for the neutralisation of the Spanish squadron at Port Mahon, the establishment of British garrisons in Majorca and Minorca, and the provision of facilities for watering and victualling His Majesty's ships.

The Captain General, Don Miguel Vives on receiving these proposals, refused to enter into any convention which involved a surrender of sovereignty and which cast doubts upon the Supreme Junta's reliability as an ally. Admiral Thornbrough was constrained therefore to inform the C. in C. in a pained despatch that, though the Captain General had asked for money, arms and ammunition as well as the protection of the fleet, he refusedto accede to the British request that part of the Spanish Squadron should be surrendered, or be laid up or join the British against the enemy. All he was prepared to give in return for British help was permission for the ships to water.

In the meantime Collingwood had received instructions from the Government not to take any offensive action against the Balearics but to give them all the assistance possible. Already Admiral Thornbrough had been warned by his prescient C. in C. that "It may be necessary to inform the Governor General of the Islands that you will aid him to repel the common enemy and leave him to ask the assistance he wants ... The Governor General of Majorca being the officer who holds the chief command in the Islands, your correspondence in what relates to the general system must be with him, in all things shewing a perfect confidence in the integrity of the Spaniards to the cause of their country."

On receiving the Captain General's flat rejection of the proposed convention, Collingwood at once sent a further letter to him promising all aid in

*On receiving news of their release Lord Collingwood immediately sent instructions to the agent for prisoners of war at Malta to release all Spanish prisoners.

defending the islands from the French and asking only in return permission for H.M. ships to water.

The ship which conveyed Admiral Collingwood's message was none other than the famous "Imperieuse", under her even more famous commander, that most radical and foudroyant of heroes and geniuses, Lord Cochrane. Frederick Marryat was also aboard, one of the midshipmen whom their formidable captain inspired to perform feats of military enterprise as daring and dashing as his own. In the "Autobiography of a Seaman" Cochrane relates, with that absence of humour often characteristic of heroes, how the citizens of Palma "were at first shy" when his ship arrived in the bay "apparently fearing some deception". They can scarcely be blamed for being "shy" in view of the fact that his Lordship, whose stratagems had become legendary along the Eastern seaboard of Spain, had been busily occupied for some months past in capturing and sinking Majorcan shipping, carrying off their cattle, sheep and - worst of all - their pigs, and blowing up forts whenever their garrisons had the temerity to announce their presence by firing at his ship. Alcudia Bay was frequently the scene of Cochrane's depradations - how right the Alcudians had been two centuries previously to be wary of the English. On one occasion when he appeared in the Bay, the "'Imperieuse' was fired upon by the small battery of Jacemal, and having subsequently reconnoitred it more closely, it appeared practicable to destroy it by a night attack. Accordingly we again ran in and soon reaching the tower blew it up, dismounting three guns. A guard house near the battery was set on fire, after which we returned to the frigate without loss. At daylight on the following morning we had the satisfaction to perceive that our work had been effectual, the whole being in ruins. As the place stood on an eminence very difficult of access, and commanding two bays, (of Pollensa and Alcudia) its demolition was desirable" ("Autobiography of a Seaman"). The dismounted guns of this fort, which was situated on the neck of the Punta de la Victoria, overlooking Mal Pas and Puerto Alcudia were still to be seen at the end of the century and very likely they are there to this day - as the place is "very difficult of access".

Lord Cochrane enjoyed his visit to Palma not only because the inhabitants were so friendly and showered presents on his ships, "payment being resolutely refused", but more especially because "we had also the satisfaction of here recovering our lost midshipman Harrison and the late Lord Napier, who, whilst in charge of prizes had been taken and carried into Port Mahon." So we have to thank the Majorcans in general and their Supreme Junta in particular for having looked after and set at liberty the original (Napier) of one of the heroes of English fiction, O'Brien, in "Peter Simple".

The Captain General was not slow to take advantage of the British Government's offer brought by Lord Cochrane and demands for money and arms were reiterated. These were required not only for the defence of Majorca, but in order to equip and train troops that were urgently needed for operations in Catalonia. Rear Admiral Martin, who had been left in charge of the British squadron in Majorcan waters, gave the Captain General all he could spare, but the shortage of money and arms was to be a persistent feature of Majorcan affairs for the next few years. As for the raising of troops to fight in metropolitan Spain, nothing was effectively done until the arrival of an energetic British Army officer named Samford Whittingham.

Lord Wellington was not quite confident that the security of the Balearic Islands could be entrusted entirely to the Royal Navy and in March 1810 he was writing to his brother Henry, "Whether the fleet is or is not sent to Minorca, the security of the Balearic Islands is a consideration of the utmost importance, which must not be lost sight of." His Lordship did not allow his anxiety to remain unallayed and in November it was decided that Colonel Whittingham should be sent to Majorca to raise what afterwards achieved considerable fame and glory and was known as the "Majorcan Division".

Samuel Ford Whittingham, known to his friends as Samford, the son of a Bristol merchant, was one of those rare Army officers who in the great age of privilege, patronage, placemen and pocket boroughs, achieved distinction without the aid of family or family connexions. That he rose to become a General and a K.C.B. was due entirely to his own efforts and very considerable talents. He joined the Army in 1803 as an Ensign at the age of thirty-one, the age at which Arthur Wellesley was already a full Colonel and the ruler of Mysore. Previously he had been in Spain looking after the Spanish end of the family business, and while there he obtained a thorough knowledge of the Spanish language. It was probably due to this that he was sent on a secret mission to Spain by Pitt the year after he joined the army. He was next sent to South America with the force that never reached Peru. Instead he found himself an extra A.D.C. to General Whitelocke, whose disastrous expedition to Buenos Aires, was only one of several planned by the Horse Guards in those years.

In 1808 he was appointed a Deputy Assistant QMG on the staff of the expeditionary force that was sent to Sicily. This appointment did not please him however and being anxious to serve where his knowledge of Spanish might be of some use, he succeeded in persuading Sir Hew Dalrymple, Governor of Gibraltar, where he stopped en route for Sicily, to allow him to join the army of the Spanish General Castaños as a volunteer. Sir Hew, who was soon to go down in history as an object of ridicule as a result of his part in the unpopular Convention of Cintra, deputed Whittingham to send him "a faithful and exact account of the Spanish Army and its activities etc." Dalrymple was one of the few senior British officers who had the vision to see the potentialities of Spanish popular resistance to the French and his detractors have seldom allowed him due credit for the encouragement and support he gave it.

The enthusiastic Whittingham, longing for active service, was soon to be satisfied and, after joining Castaños, he shared in that General's memorable victory over the French at Bailen, where he achieved the distinction of being the first British officer to be actively engaged in the Peninsular War. After Castaños had relinquished his command, Whittingham was attached as British Military Agent to the Duke of Albuquerque. He was wounded at the Battle of Talavera and it was while recovering from his wound at Seville that he met and married, appropriately enough as it turned out, a lady whose family had been connected with Majorca and Minorca since the days of Jaime the Conquistador. Also while he was at Seville, Whittingham saw a lot of his friends John Hookham Frere, the British Minister and his brother Bartholomew, commonly known as Bartle. This friendship led to a brief and tragic romance, for Bartle fell in love with Whittingham's sister-in-law, married her by proxy, when he was at Constantinople and received the news of her death by the ship that should have brought herself.

It was during this convalescent period at Seville that Whittingham seems to have first considered the possibility of going to the Balearic Islands. In April 1810 soon after Wellington had expressed concern about their defence, he was writing to his brother-in-law, Hart Davis, the member for Bristol, that he was thinking of requesting General Castaños to make him Inspector General of the troops in the Balearics, particularly if his former chief, the Duke of Albuquerque should become Captain General. Three months later he informed the same correspondent that he intended to propose to the Government that he should raise a corps of 2,000 cavalry in Majorca and by November of that year the proposal had been accepted and he himself appointed to the sole direction of it. It was not, however, until June 1811 that Whittingham arrived at Palma with his assistant Colonel Patrick Campbell. Almost exactly a year later they left again having created in that short period the famous "Majorca Division", which was to win glory in some of the final campaigns of the Peninsular War.

It was a remarkable achievement when the enormous difficulties with which Whittingham had to contend, are considered. In the first place the Captain General of the Balearics at that time was none other than that notorious old anglophobe, General Gregorio Cuesta, whose co-operation the Iron Duke had once begged for on bended knee, and who harboured a particular dislike for "Don Santiago" Whittingham. But General Cuesta was not the only person in Majorca, hostile to the British. There was also an influential body of opinion that was strongly pro-French. This was drawn chiefly from the ranks of the descendants of the "Butifarras". "Butifarra"* or in Catalan "Botifarra", meaning a large sausage, was the term of abuse applied to those members of the Majorcan nobility, who sided with the Bourbons in the War of the Spanish Succession. No doubt many of them were members of the Sociedad Económica, who had feared that their reforms and all hope of further enlightenment might be jeopardised if Ferdinand VII were to be restored to the throne of Spain. That the French faction could not by any means be disregarded was illustrated by their plot to subvert the "Majorca Division" when Whittingham happened to be three weeks in Minorca. Moreover eight or nine thousand French prisoners of war taken at Bailen, whose repatriation had been prevented by the British, were slowly starving and dying of disease on the barren island of Cabrera, some ten miles off the nearest point of Majorca, and they and their officers, many of whom on Whittingham's arrival were still at large in Palma itself, were a perpetual source of danger to Allied security. Whittingham urged that the officers should be sent to Port Mahon, but they were finally compelled to join their unfortunate fellow prisoners on Cabrera. Even those Majorcans who were supposed to be most attached to the Anglo-Spanish alliance were often far from co-operative. The Supreme Junta, for example, at first refused to supply the Division with fodder for the horses and the Spanish War Minister, out of jealousy for Whittingham's privileged position, which exempted him from control by Spanish inspectors, was constantly putting obstacles in his path.

*I am indebted to Robert Graves for a most ingenious derivation of the word "Botifarra" which I believe is still used in much the same way as "Blimp" is used in English. He suggested that *Botulus* (Latin for sausage) + *farcer* ("to stuff") got connected with an old limouisine word for esquire - "one who shined up his lord's boots (*farder* + *bottes*) and that "Botifarra" meaning a sausage is a corruption of "Botifarra" meaning a gent. So that "Sausage" is named after a certain kind of gent, and not the other way round (c.f. "stuffed shirt").

But he had powerful allies, foremost among whom was the Bishop of Majorca. This prelate's enthusiasm for Whittingham's undertaking extended so far as to afford him practical assistance in the form of money and a house for the establishment of a school for the officers and cadets of the Division. With the Bishop so uncompromisingly on his side, Whittingham could count on the support of most of the clergy and through them, of the faithful populace, which had already shown itself to be violently hostile to the French. The Francophobia of the Church seems to have been so violent that even the confessional box was pressed into service in order to provide "Don Santiago" with red-hot intelligence. Finally the two Majorcan representatives in the Cortes at Cadiz were whole-heartedly in favour of Whittingham and they and the Bishop went so far as to desire that he should become Governor of Majorca, the actual incumbent of that office being in their view too "attached to French principles".

In adition to his native allies there was now always Sir Edward Pellew at Port Mahon to be appealed to. That distinguished officer, better known perhaps as Lord Exmouth, was always ready to help with supplies when all other sources failed.

In spite of the ardent patriotism of the Majorcan people there was scarcely a rush of volunteers to join a corps, which was generally understood to be destined for service on the mainland. Whittingham was therefore hard put to find enough recruits and it is a tribute to the regard in which he was generally held by the islanders, that he succeeded finally in raising a regiment of sharpshooters from among them. The remaining units were composed of refugees from the provinces of Cordoba and Murcia and six hundred Germans who had been taken prisoner at Bailen and who were no doubt delighted to exchange the near certainty of death by starvation on Cabrera, for the slightly better fed hazards of service with the "Majorca Division".

By February 1812 the Division consisted of 2,200 men but as there was no money to pay them, Whittingham had to report that they were almost starving. In April, Wellington, optimistically reckoning that the strength of the Division would soon be brought up to 7,000, was contemplating employing it on the mainland. Whittingham a month later hoped to have 5,000 men under his command if he could get Sir E. Pellew to feed some of them. Finally, on July 24th, 1812, the Division embarked at Palma for the Peninsula. It consisted of cavalry and artillery and an infantry force of 159 officers, 3 chaplains, 8 surgeons and 4,180 non-commissioned officers and men.

In the campaigns of 1812 and 1813 the Division covered itself with glory and its proud commander, writing home to Hart Davis in October 1812, informed him that "the Majorca Division has the honour of occupying all the outposts of the army." In January 1813 much to his relief, Whittingham was told that in future the Division would be paid by the British Government so that his prinicpal worry from that date was, not to find the money, but to account for it, a task which he sometimes felt was beyond him. The Division greatly distinguished itself at the battle of Castalla, when Marshal Suchet was defeated by the allied army under Sir John Murray, and Whittingham's reputation was vastly enhancedl. He was already a Lieutenant General in the Spanish Army and two years later Ferdinand VII, who respected and liked him, invited him to become Minister of War, an offer which he declined on the advice of Lord Castlereagh. By August 1815, the "Majorca Division", having grown to eight battalions of infantry, two regiments of cavalry and two troops of horse artillery was raised to the status of a *corps d'armée*. It was at this point that Whittingham resigned the command and returned to England. He later became Governor of Dominica in the West Indies and finally C. in C. of the Madras Presidency, where he died in 1841.

Majorcan opinion and appreciation of England and things English had never been higher than they were during the Peninsular War. The Sociedad Económica had introduced English literature, English (and Scotch) political economy, English biscuits and English potatoes, all of which were apparently much esteemed. Colonel Whittingham introduced English military discipline and educational methods, which were perhaps slightly less welcome. People were learning to speak English and about the time that the "Majorca Division" was being formed, an enterprising tailor was initiating the unsophisticated citizens of Palma into the elegant extravagance of London fashions. This was a sign of the times, for in an atmosphere of war and revolution, the rancid society of Palma was becoming worldly, liberal and frivolous. Opera was much in vogue and the people were flocking to Cimarosa's "Il Matrimonio Segreto" and the enchanting works of Paesiello. Some devotees of those delectable profanities so far forgot themselves that it is on record that they were heard to sing in the street a popular number from Paesiello's "Barber of Seville".

Enthusiasm for the English reached a climax, when the entry of the Allies into Madrid was celebrated at a gala night at the Palma theatre on August 26th 1812. A special programme was designed for the occasion by the poets and dramatists of Palma, who produced the lyrics, sketches and tableaux within twenty-four hours. It can hardly have been a very polished performance but popular acclaim was not to be diminished because of blemishes due to under-rehearsal. The entertainment was entitled "Loa en Celebridad de la Libertad de Madrid" and the dramatis personae included Madrid, whose part was taken by one Barbara Fort, Wellington, Empecinado, Don Carlos of Spain and "a Portuguese General".

The lion's part was taken of course by Wellington, who asks Madrid "to permit an honourable English military man to be the first to break the chain that perfidy has placed upon her and to kiss her hand." Madrid, overcome with gratitude, tries to kneel but is prevented from doing so by her chivalrous deliverer. She then praises the "proud (but nameless) Lusitanian", while Don Carlos gets a pat on the back from the "English military man". Empecinado seems to have been left out in this preliminary round of mutual congratulation.

The final scene depicts the enthroning of Madrid. The unknown Portuguese General covers her shoulders with the Royal Mantle, Don Carlos hands her the sceptre and Wellington places the crown on her head. At last Empecinado is allowed to have his say and delivers himself of an impassioned epilogue:

*Viva Espana, viva, viva*
*Viva, siendo en todos deuda*
*Y obligacion, aplaudir*
*Las Britanicas banderas*
*Como nuestros protectores*
       *(Todos)*
*Viva, y felices se vean.*

Long live Spain, viva, viva,
Viva and let all feel the debt
And obligation owed and applaud
The British standards
As our protectors
      (All)
Long life and happiness to everyone.

But everyone was not destined to be so very happy and some lived less long than they might, for the Restoration brought in its train repression and the Inquisition, the latter being welcomed by many a rancid Majorcan as a sedative after their heady indulgence in the pagan distractions of Italian opera. Wellington, having departed behind the Pyrenees, was no longer the hero of the hour. Instead irritation was being felt with his younger brother Lord Cowley for intervening on behalf of Spanish liberals suffering persecution under Ferdinand's regime, many of whom were exiled in Majorca. It is satisfactory to record that Cowley was successful in shaming the deplorable Ferdinand into revoking the sentence of death passed on one liberal imprisoned in Majorca, to whom the Royal amnesty had previously been promised.

# CHAPTER VII
## PALMA CATHEDRAL AND THE MARQUIS DE LA ROMANA

*... in him the Spanish army had lost its brightest ornament: his country its most upright patriot; and the world the most strenuous defender of the cause of liberty.*
The Duke of Wellington on the Marquis de la Romana

Churches may be divided into two main categories; those which inspire a feeling of religious awe and those which do not. To the second category belong national shrines, such as Westminster Abbey and, though much less obviously, Notre Dame, where secular associations are so powerful that one sometimes has the impression that God has been left to play second fiddle to Caesar. In the first category perhaps the supreme example is Chartres Cathedral, with Palma very little inferior to it. In both of these great churches it would surely be difficult not to experience some sensation, however slight, of other-worldliness, not to feel that their builders were inspired, if not from on high, at least by an ideal that transcended purely temporal considerations. This does not, of course, mean that the founders of Westminster Abbey were at all less pious than the founders of Palma Cathedral, that Edward the Confessor and Henry III were worse Christians than Jaime the Conqueror, but sensations of awe and reverence aroused by a great building do not necessarily have any reference to historical fact. The visitor to Westminster Abbey is apt to be overwhelmed, in spite of himself, by the obtrusive presence of the stone and plaster and bronze images and other memorials of England's greatest sons. His emotions tend to be patriotic and imperial and the Deity becomes confused with a sentimental trinity of St George, Sir Edward Elgar and Rudyard Kipling.

It is otherwise with Palma Cathedral, in which Majorcan efforts to invest it with the attributes of a national shrine have completely failed to obscure or diminish its glory as a monument and symbol of Christendom. When I visited it, I was not unprepared for the experience, since all who have written about this great church have testified in their fashion to its inspiring qualities, which Havelock Ellis briefly analysed in "The Soul of Spain". Much of the awe that filled me on entering sprang probably from the sheer immensity of the interior. There are larger churches than Palma cathedral but the colossal emptiness of its nave is unique. Though the dimensions of the nave of Gerona cathedral are slightly larger, its size is apparently diminished by the fabric of the choir it contains. The nave of Milan cathedral, usually ranked as the third largest church in the world, is a few inches higher, but it less wide. The uninterrupted cubic area of the nave of Palma cathedral is in fact unparalleled in any religious building. Within it could be enclosed Westminster Abbey or Notre Dame or York Minster. The width of the naves of these churches is thirty-eight feet, forty-eight feet and fifty-two feet respectively, whereas the nave of Palma cathedral is no less than a hundred and eighty feet wide. Its roof in which owls have their nests is ten feet higher than the roof of the Albert Hall and it is more than half as long as St Pancras Station, which is a formerly odorous but still useful comparison.

Another circumstance that rendered my visit to the Cathedral memorable was to some extent fortuitous. A wedding was in progress and throughout the ceremony the organ was being gently played and the whole of the great building was filled with its soft sweet tones. The excellence of this organ has been noted by other observers and I have no doubt that it contributed powerfully to the holinessof the Cathedral.

The success of a building as a place of spiritual exaltation, or indeed for most purposes, depends of course very largely on its lighting, and in this respect Palma cathedral is triumphant. It is neither too dark like Seville Cathedral, where one feels the need of an electric torch, nor too light as in churches where mysteries are eschewed and nothing is left to the imagination of the unimaginative. Daylight is admitted by plain glass windows high up on the South front and also by the brightly coloured rose windows in the apse. The artificial lighting, so often the ruin of large interiors, is well adjusted to augment and enhance the light from the windows, particularly the "brightly lighted little apse, high up, which is charmingly effective", noted by Havelock Ellis, and which blends well with the rose windows above.

I lingered in the Cathedral until the wedding was over, when the great West doors were thrown open and the slender couple walked down the full length of the nave upon a thin red carpet, to the familiar forced cheerfulness of Mendelssohn's Wedding March, towards a flood of extra light. It was all most moving, and I doubt if there is a more impressive and magnificent setting for a marriage ceremony.

Though the Majorcans do look upon Palma Cathedral as their Westminster Abbey, they have not succeeded in transforming it literally into a national shrine. Their efforts in this direction have indeed sometimes produced a contrary effect. To gaze at dead of night upon the ghastly remains of a Majorcan monarch, deceased more than six hundred years ago, is likely to induce distrust rather than veneration of princes. Perhaps that is why this macabre privilege has been withdrawn. King Jaime is now suffered to lie undisturbed beneath one of the few memorial stones the Cathedral contains.

Of these the most important is one which might with equal propriety be accorded a niche in the Abbey, for the dominant if not the central figure is none other than the Duke of Wellington. He is represented, and quite recognisably, standing by the death bed of the Spanish general and Majorcan nobleman, Pedro Caro y Sureda, Marquis de la Romana. This somewhat unexpected grouping came about as the result of one of the most exciting and dramatic episodes in the Napoleonic Wars.

The story of the adventure properly begins in the eleventh century, when a number of monasteries were founded in Germany by Benedictine monks, who had been expelled from Ireland or Scotland. By the end of the eighteenth century, two at least of these monasteries were still in existence, one at Erfurt and the other at Ratisbon. To the latter foundation there had subsequently been attached a seminary for Scotch candidates for the priesthood and one of the teachers at this seminary was a certain James Robertson.

It seems that the monks, true to the tradition of their Order, were in the habit of extending a hospitable welcome to any gentlemen on the Grand Tour, who happened to call on them. Among the many travellers who received such hospitality in return for the pleasure their company gave to expatriates too much dependent on their own, was the Duke of Richmond, who later became Viceroy of Ireland. During his Viceroyalty, Robertson, who was then living in Dublin, made himself known to the Duke, reminded him of Ratisbon days and offered his services to the Government in any capacity that "would not disgrace his cloth". The Duke commended the Benedictine to Sir Arthur Wellesley, at that time Chief Secretary for Ireland, and as a result Robertson was summoned to an interview from which he emerged, he later wrote, with the consciousness that he had been in the presence of a "master spirit, gifted with a capacity to make all time become his own." Sir Arthur seems also to have been favourably impressed by the Roman Catholic priest, to whom he gave employment as a confidential agent in Dublin. Not long afterwards the Chief Secretary was to be instrumental in his protege being entrusted by the British Government with a mission of extreme delicacy and importance.

Under the terms of the Treaty of Basle, which the Spanish Prime Minister Godoy had concluded with Napoleon, Spain undertook to furnish fourteen thousand troops for service with the Imperial armies. Accordingly, in May 1807 a number of Spanish regiments marched across Spain and France to Northern Germany, where they were joined by further contingents from Tuscany. The whole force was placed under the command of the Marquis de la Romana and formed part of the army of Marshal Bernadotte. Its original task was to protect the mouths of the Elbe and Weser, but it was later sent to the Danish Isles to form the spearhead of the proposed invasion of Sweden. It was at this juncture that the Spanish people rose against the usurpation of the Spanish monarchy by Joseph Bonaparte, and, on hearing the news of the uprising, the British Government decided that efforts should be made to secure the defection of or at least to neutralise the Spanish troops under the Marquis de la Romana.

The French were naturally not by any means confident of the loyalty of Romana and his troops and Bernadotte's suspicions were increased when the Spanish general made his allegiance to King Joseph conditional on Joseph's assumption of the throne being accepted by the unanimous consent of the Spanish people. Measures were therefore taken to insulate Romana and his men from all authentic news of events in Spain and postal communication with their home land was completely severed.

The problem before the British Government was to find a means to acquaint Romana with the true state of affairs in Spain, and to offer him the opportunity of defecting. In doing this it was vital both to avoid compromising him with the French and to convince him of the authenticity of the message. It was not an easy problem and the British Government brought it as they were to bring many other problems for the next forty years or more to Arthur Wellesley to solve. The "master spirit" was not at a loss: indeed he must have welcomed the approach for he was at that moment hatching a scheme for a campaign in the Peninsula, having just received the report of a spy he had sent to Spain. The answer to the Government's problem, he concluded, was to be found in the Romish priest, whom he had recently left behind in Ireland. There was a man, who not only spoke perfect German and had proved himself in Ireland as a reliable confidential agent, but who had expressed an ardent wish to be employed by His Majesty's Government. Now was the time to give him his chance.

Robertson was summoned to London, a summons that he instantly obeyed. He need not have been so prompt, for the Foreign Office had evidently not made up its mind and weeks went by without any further reference to the employment Sir Arthur had promised him on his arrival in London. In despair the priest engaged himself as Private Chaplain to a Roman Catholic peer, the Earl of Shrewsbury, but no sooner had this pleasant appointment been confirmed, than he received a further summons to the Irish Office. There the nature of the job the Government had in mind for him was explained by Wellesley. Robertson accepted it and he was formally engaged on the same day, May 31st, 1808. The following day Sir Arthur wrote his appreciation of "the plan of operations at present in contemplation", which probably decided Ministers to send a British expeditionary force to Spain.

On the 4th June Robertson left London for Heligoland via Harwich, in the company of a Foreign Office official named Mackenzie, who was empowered to treat with the Marquis de la Romana. On the same day Ministers were talking of Sir Arthur Wellesley for the command in the Peninsula. Robertson reached Heligoland on June 6th, the day that Castlereagh approved Sir Arthur's "plan", and Consul Nicholas arranged for him to be landed on the island of Neuwerk at the mouth of the Elbe three days later. In spite of a letter to the Governor, with which he had been provided, Robertson's arrival in the island was not welcomed. The islanders were in such a state of terror after a recent visit from the French, when every bed in the island had been searched that they begged him to depart at once and, having spent an uneasy night ashore, he returned to Heligoland.

This experience had thoroughly alarmed him and he now felt inclined to abandon the whole enterprise as being much too dangerous. Mackenzie however gave him a strong "pep talk" after which he declared himself ready once more to make the attempt.

The resourceful Nicholas was again asked to provide means for landing the emissary on the shores of a hostile Continent and on June 12th Robertson left Heligoland for the second time in a vessel belonging to one Bukemeyer, a German merchant who, like many others, had been forced by Napoleon's "Continental System" to turn smuggler. The following day, after an anxious night of false alarms at the mouth of the Weser and having successfully passed through a heavily bribed French customs post, Robertson was safely deposited at Herr Bukemeyer's residence at Bremen.

His situation was not however a happy one for he had no identity papers nor any means by which to justify his presence in Bremen, should he be questioned by the French or German authorities. Though arrangements for controlling the movements of aliens and unauthorised visitors were inevitably less comprehensive and effective in the days before the typewriter, the camera and electronic communications than they are now, it is almost incredible that the Foreign Office should have despatched a secret agent on a highly important and hazardous mission, without providing him with some protection or disguise. Yet it seems that Robertson had to depend entirely on his own initiative to secure the necessary credentials that would enable him to pursue his journey through occupied Europe, unmolested and unsuspected. Though the Foreign Office did not provide him with travel documents, they did furnish him with something with which, given initiative, they might possibly be procured. He had plenty of money. Sewn into the lining of his pocket book, was a letter of credit on Hamburg to the value of £100.

In describing in his narrative the means he employed to obtain convincing credentials, Robertson confesses with charming ingenuousness that they were "at variance with the strict rule of veracity, but," he argues, "they seemed allowable considering the object they were to serve." His duplicity was not after all so very base, and would scarcely have caused a qualm in a more experienced intelligence operator. All he did was to adopt the name of a friend of about his own age, who had left Germany many years previously and all of whose close relations were dead. He applied for a passport in this man's name and had it duly visaed by the French authorities. In order to make his credentials doubly sure, he obtained from the parish priest a certificate of his friend's baptism.

Robertson reached Hamburg on June 19th and, having cashed his bill of exchange, completed his preparations for the journey to Romana's headquarters. The role of commercial traveller seemed to him the one best suited to his purpose and accordingly he laid in a stock of chocolate and fine cigars, for which he knew Spaniards have a special liking. He also procured letters of introduction to merchants at Lubeck, presumably from the Hamburg merchant on whom his bill of exchange had been drawn.

While in Hamburg he had made known the real object of his journey to two Spaniards at the Altona military depot, from whom he hoped, though in vain, to obtain help in the execution of his mission. He was however able to send a letter in covert language to Mackenzie in Heligoland, probably through the agency of Bukemeyer or one of his friends.

Robertson left Hamburg on June 21st and, travelling via Lubeck, Kiel and Assens eventually reached Romana's headquarters at Nyborg in the Danish island of Funen. There he succeeded without much difficulty in obtaining a private interview with the Spanish commander, ostensibly for the purpose of displaying his luxury wares. Having secured this interview, his next task was to convince Romana that he was indeed the bearer of a message from the British Government. As it was considered too dangerous for him to possess written credentials, a scheme by which he hoped to prove his bona fides orally had been devised. It depended on Romana's close and long standing friendship with John Hookham Frere, whom he had known when the latter was British Ambassador in Madrid. Years later Frere said of him "Romana and I were friends from the very first day we met." How close the friendship was may perhaps be indicated by the language of the following note he once received:

Dearest Friend,
My bosom and heart is enticed for you, and I pray you to expect me.
Your in all devoted friend,
M. de la Romana.

It had been decided that an incident which occurred when they were alone together and which would be unknown to anyone else, but which Romana would probably remember, should be Robertson's password. Authorities differ on the incident chosen by Frere and the one most favoured and repeated in almost every account of the adventure including Wellington's, is concerned with Frere's suggested correction of a line in Corneille's tragedy "Le Cid". Robertson, however, who was the person most likely to know, says that he was instructed to remind the Marquis "that the first time he (Frere) had the pleasure of dining with you was at Toledo. After dinner you withdrew together into a cabinet containing books. In this cabinet there was one picture. That picture was by Mengs, and represented St Peter and St John at the gate of the Temple." Romana recollected the incident and recognised also a sample of Frere's handwriting that Robertson had brought with him.

Having successfully established his identity, Robertson delivered his message which was that the Spanish people were in revolt against the French invader and that if Romana and his troops were prepared either to join in the struggle or at least to withdraw their support for Napoleon, the British Government would be pleased to transport them to Spain or South America or to the Marquis's native island of Majorca.

Romana refused to give Robertson an answer either at this time or at a second interview. The emissary was on the point of leaving Nyborg, having narrowly escaped arrest, when Romana summoned him a third time and announced his intention of accepting the British Government's proposal. Robertson left at once to send the good news to London and having reached Hamburg safely "embraced the opportunity offered me of writing to Mr Mackenzie at Heligoland to report the successful accomplishment of my mission and to request that instructions might be sent to the commander of the British fleet in the Baltic to hold themselves in readiness to communicate with the Spanish General."

Robertson's letter must have reached Mackenzie about July 20th and as soon as the Foreign Office received the news, instructions were sent to Admiral Keats, who commanded the squadron operating round the Danish Isles, to "open communication" with Romana. Meanwhile a Spanish officer had already defected, though apparently without instructions from the General and, having been picked up by one of the ships in Keats's squadron, had described the true state of feeling among the Spanish troops. Three days later, on August 5th, just two months since Robertson had left England on his eventful mission, Admiral Keats sent a letter to the officers of His Most Catholic Majesty's troops conveying the British Government's offer of evacuation. Romana, who was of course expecting such a message, had already taken secret measures to enable him to accept the offer and four days later almost the entire Spanish contingent, numbering nearly twelve thousand men was safely evacuated. They were subsequently transported to Spain, where two months later they were nearly all killed at the disastrous battle of Epinosa.

For his part in the evacuation Admiral Keats was awarded the K.C.B. Robertson also in Wellington's opinion "received the fair reward of his courage and discretion and was well provided for by the British Government." This reward consisted of a cash payment of £1,000 of which he received in fact only £900, £100 having already been paid to his family before his return to England, a year after the successful outcome of his mission. His delay in returning was due to the impossibility of obtaining a passage to Heligoland, without being apprehended by the French authorities, whose security measures had been tightened as a result of Romana's escape. In order that they might abandon the search for him, Robertson asked that the English newspapers should be told that he had returned safely to England. This was not done however, and Robertson, in despair of making a get-away from the Continent, at least for the time being, decided he would be safer if he left the frontier areas.

Ratisbon seemed the obvious place to make for, since he could certainly count on every assistance from his former colleagues at the Scotch College. Moreover he was unlikely to be molested, travelling as he would be, towards the heart of Germany. His route took him through Jena whose recently stricken field claimed another casualty in the fugitive secret agent. Meditating too deeply upon the famous victory, Robertson stumbled, fell and badly bruised a knee. He hobbled on to Erfurt where Napoleon was then receiving the unwilling respects of the Princes of Europe. Robertson, who had once met the Emperor, did not seek to renew the acquaintance but stayed quietly at the Scotch monastery, a sister foundation of the one at Ratisbon.

After a few weeks at Ratisbon, he went on to Linz, where he stayed with a former colleague. From Linz he paid a flying visit to Munich in order to distribute leaflets giving the news of the French setbacks in Spain. He escaped from Bavaria only by the skin of his teeth and when Austria was invaded he was obliged to flee again. This time there was nothing for it but to retrace his steps across Germany. Here Napoleon almost caught up with him and his post chaise was pursued by dragoons all the way from Dresden to Cuxhaven, where he embarked for England. It is not surprising in the circumstances, that he did not feel disposed to dally in Hamburg in order to cash a bill of exchange for the £900 that the Foreign Office had somehow succeeded in sending there "to await his arrival".

Robertson was not content with this reward and wrote several times to George Canning and then to Earl Bathurst, who succeeded him for a short time as Foreign Secretary. He recalled the sacrifices and dangers he had endured in the accomplishment of his mission, pointed out the impossibility of living on the interest of £900, and requested that the Government should give him some further employment. His letters remained unanswered and the man, who had chiefly been responsible for the happy outcome of the operation that was considered at the time to be even more important than the Spanish victory at Bailen, was left to shift for himself in neglected obscurity. Abandoning hope of securing any official employment he returned to Ireland, but in 1813 the Foreign Office seem to have repented of their meanness and sent him on another mission. He was in Paris for the entry of the Allies in 1815, after which he retired to the Scotch monastery at Ratisbon, where he died five years later. (The monastery steadily declined in wealth and size after the Napoleonic Wars and by 1840 only two monks were left and five young Scotch candidates for the priesthood. It was finally suppressed in 1862, but the building continued to be used as a seminary until the Second World War.)

Romana returned to Spain after his escape from Denmark and received a triumphal welcome from the people of Madrid, who drew his carriage through the streets, "an honour never bestowed upon a person in Spain before" asserted Lady Holland. The evacuation of the Spanish troops from Denmark, which according to the Spanish historian, Menendez y Pelayo, "was as marvellous as the one recorded by Xenophon", had made a great impression in Spain and throughout Europe. A year later it was still a popular topic and Lady Holland, when she went to a splendid illumination at the theatre at Cadiz in honour of George III, saw "a representation of the escape of Romana and his army from the Isle of Funen." "A dull performance however," she decided.

Romana's next experience of collaboration with the English was disastrous. As C. in C. of the Spanish Army of Galicia, he sought to co-operate with Sir John Moore, but that impatient and undiplomatic hero who "placed no dependence on him (Romana) or his army" was not the man to try and understand the point of view of his Spanish ally, much less to fit in with his plans, which he dismissed as absurdly unrealistic. For his part Romana, who found Sir John's handwriting difficult to read, rightly or wrongly "in the gentlest terms ascribed the ruin and dispersion of his army to Sir John Moore having deceived him." He bore no malice however and after Corunna, any resentment he may have felt evaporated in generous admiration for his brave if unsympathetic ally and the monument over the grave of Sir John Moore at Corunna was erected at his initiative.

Eighteen months later it fell to another English general, with whom Romana's relations had been happier, to repay the compliment, and early in 1811 Lord Wellington was making arrangements for the suitable disposal of his friend's remains. The Duke, who shared Moore's low opinion of Romana's military talents, valued what the lesser man failed to appreciate and admired the little Majorcan as a patriot and a loyal ally. Writing of him to the Spanish Prime Minister, Mendizabal, shortly after his illness and death, the Duke expressed himself with unwonted feeling, "I have lost a colleague, a friend and an adviser with whom I had lived on the happiest terms of friendship, intimacy and confidence: and I shall revere and regret his memory to the last moment of my existence."

Another and not less endearing character of Romana as a man and a higher estimation of him as a soldier came from the archæologist and traveller Sir William Gell - Byron's "rapid Gell" because he wrote a book about Troy after spending only three days on the site. Gell met Romana in Portugal not long before his death and in a letter dated 9 November 1810 to Horace Walpole's unhappy love, Mary Berry, he described the impression the Marquis had made on him. He was "quite astonished to find how well, first of all, he talks English, and afterwards, what a fund of information, not to say learning, the little wretch has. I talked a great deal to him, and called on him the next morning. As to his figure, such a gig was never seen - a little yellow tailor, smothered in waistcoat lapels, with a blue coat bordered with broad gold lace, very full at top, and coming below to a very narrow waist, the picture of one's great-grandfather. He is very lively and good-humoured, and entirely without humbug."

In a letter dated 2 February 1811 to the same correspondent Gell wrote of Romana's death. "Romana is dead, and we went in procession to his burial. He was, perhaps, the only learned man in his country, and I believe the only person in the Peninsula who had information sufficient to guide his judgment beyond the mere events of the day. He was a very good scholar - a thing quite unheard of in Spain; he was very well read in history, and if he was not a good general, which I very much doubt, there is no hope of a better among the survivors. Moreover, a person who with a small army and confined resources can preserve himself from any serious defeat with 20,000 enemies in the country, for the space of two years, cannot be so very bad a commander as the English would represent him. I took particular pains to get acquainted with him, and think I never saw a person of whom one has heard so much, with so little of the humbug grandissima about him."

The memorial in Palma Cathedral, which was erected in 1811 on the orders of the Cortes of Cadiz, is not only symbolical of a close and friendly collaboration but depicts literally its final scene, when Romana died in Portugal on January 23rd, 1811. Many years later the Duke, speaking of the Marquis, told Lord Mahon that he "was a good natured, excellent man, most easy to live with, and very clever, too - knew all about the literature and poetry of his country more than any Spaniard I ever knew, but he knew nothing of troops at all. I never in my whole life saw a man, who had acted with troops at all, understand so little about them. I liked him very much - he died in my arms - at least I was in the room at the time; but as to his generalship—."

It is appropriate that this friendship should be commemorated in Palma Cathedral where many thousands may see the memorial and perhaps be reminded of the ties which once bound England with Spain.

# CHAPTER VIII
## MAJORCA AND THE ENGLISH

The history of England's association with Majorca is long and mostly happy, which may be why it has remained unwritten until now. It begins in the year 1232 with the arrival at Palma of one Sebastian Robes, a graduate of Oxford University, who came with a party of monks from Lerida to found in Majorca a monastery of Trinitarians. Nothing more is known about Robes, but his mission was evidently successful for the Trinitarians flourished in Palma for six centuries. It was after all a suitable place for the establishment of a house belonging to an Order, whose exclusive task was the redemption of captives and particularly of Christians in Moslem slavery, the fate of so many Majorcans.

Sebastian Robes's visit was returned some seventy years later by a Majorcan friar, who was none other than the famous Ramon Lull, known to the English as Raymond Lully. The facts of the greatest Majorcan's visit to England are obscure and some have even doubted whether he came here at all. The best authorities are, however, prepared to accept that he did come to London, probably at the invitation of Edward II, but they reject the legend that the purpose of his visit was to practise alchemy and to transmute the baser metals into gold at the request of his royal patron, allegedly in order to finance a Crusade.

In the Middle Ages when Palma was a prosperous centre of Mediterranean trade in wool, cloth, heathen slaves and many other commodities, the Majorcans exported olive oil to England and in return received cloth and Cornish tin. The ships that carried the cargoes were mainly Genoese and Venetian but sometimes an English "carrick", sailing out of Southampton would make the long voyage through the Straits of Gibraltar to Majorca and the Italian ports. In 1343 Peter I of Aragon concluded with Edward III of England an agreement regulating Anglo-Majorcan trade. That such a treaty should have been found necessary suggests that there must have been a considerable traffic between the two kingdoms and it has even been stated, though almost certainly erroneously, that an English Lonja or Exchange was established at Palma.

From the middle of the XVIth century some of the "tall ships of London" engaged in the Levant trade used occasionally to call at Majorca and the reception that one of them had from the islanders is one of the less happy episodes in the history of Anglo-Majorcan relations. Richard Hakluyt's account of the voyage of the "Susan", which bore Her Majesty's Ambassador to the Sultan of Turkey, contains possibly the first description in English of a visit to Majorca. On the 1st February 1582 the ship put into Porto Pedro in the South East corner of the island, "where we thought we might have bene as bold as in other places of Christendom." In this they were disappointed for the Majorcans on this occasion did not behave very civilly.

The first person the "Susan's" men met was a shepherd whom they entertained on board. Encouraged by the apparent friendliness both of the shepherd and other inhabitants of the port, the ship's Purser visited a neighbouring town, probably Santanyi, where he was able to purchase some provisions. The following day the Purser and several of the passengers paid another visit to the town and were promptly arrested. The Purser was sent to Palma, where he was "examined by the Viceroy very straightly" about the ship's business. Those who remained in custody at Santanyi were also interrogated by a Priest and one of them, who happened to be French, was allowed to return to the ship with a message that the Viceroy would like to come aboard.

Some days later two emissaries arrived from His Excellency - "lusty men and very well horsed" - who invited the Captain to state his wants and promised that his men should be returned to him. The English, who observed suspicious activity among the trees along the shore, were sceptical of these fair words and the Ambassador sent a letter to the Viceroy "desiring him to send his men, and not to trouble him in his voyage for he had given him no such cause nor any of his." Two days later there was another fruitless parley and the Majorcans took advantage of the delay to bring up artillery with which they were able to command the entrance of the harbour. At this point the Ambassador decided that he would have to abandon his men and get away from Majorca before it was too late. Anchor was therefore weighed and as the ship passed the entrance of the harbour, "our whole noise of trumpets were sounding on the poope with drumme and flute, and a minion of brasse on the summer decke, with two or three other pieces, always by our Gunners traversed mouth to mouth by theirs on land, still looking when they on land would shoot, for to answer them again."

The day was so calm that the ship's pilot was able to hail the shore. His shout of defiance and all the other noises from the "Susan" were answered by the Viceroy himself, who urged that they should wait to receive his letter, which he waved in his hand. The English ignored the appeal and held on until they were safely outside the harbour, where they waited in the hope that those detained might yet be released. Their patience was rewarded and after three hours their shipmates were restored safe and sound.

The Viceroy in his letter, which they brought with them, apologised for all that had taken place and explained that "injury that was offered was due to the request of the Shepheards and poore people of the countrey, for the more safeguard of their flocks, and because it was not a thing usuall to have any such shippe to come into that port." The Viceroy gave an assurance that the ship would be welcome in any other port of the Island, but the English felt that he was not to be trusted and sailed away.

The incident was typical of the state of extreme suspicion that existed in those days between England and Spain and the Majorcans were not entirely to be blamed for their mild treachery. Highly exaggerated stories of English frightfulness must have been current among the "poore people of the countrey", so that the Viceroy can hardly be blamed for taking a few precautionary measures.

Some years after the visit of the "Susan", the fears of the shepherd amd his friends were largely justified when an English fleet blockaded Majorca. The municipal authorities of Alcudia became so agitated that they sent an emissary to Philip II to point out the danger to "the most faithful city" and to beg that the fortifications might be strengthened at the expense of the Spanish Government. As a result of these representations, to which emphasis must have been given the following year by Essex and Raleigh's sack of Cadiz, an outer wall was built around the original wall, both of which by a pleasant historical accident, became many years later the private property of an Englishman.

By the beginning of the XVIIth century trade with England, in spite of wars, seems to have become sufficiently important for the British Government to consider appointing a Vice-Consul at Palma. As early as 1604 we hear of a certain Juan Perez Florian who got himself made Consul of the English against the express orders of His Britannic Majesty. Whether someone else was appointed in his stead is not known, and nothing more is recorded of a British consulate at Palma for more than sixty years until 1667, when an exequator for one Gabriel Cortes was granted. Señor Cortes was a local merchant and a member of the leading Jewish family in Majorca. His appointment as British Consul is one of the most curious events in the history of Anglo-Majorcan relations.

In 1656 the Jews were invited by Cromwell to return to England and the first few families from Amsterdam, led by the famous Manasseh ben Israel were soon well established in the City of London. Eleven years later in the year that Señor Cortes became British Consul at Palma, the Jews of Majorca, some of whom had tried to escape to England, were in communication with the Jews of London and it is more than probable that the new consul owed his appointment to this correspondence. Because of their financial skill, strong commercial sense and above all because of their comparative detachment from the politics of the countries where they lived, the Jews were frequently employed by the British Government on its business abroad. The appointment of a prominent Jew as His Majesty's representative in Majorca was not, however, entirely satisfactory and it is perhaps an indication of how little was then known in England about the island. Whatever the reasons of expediency for such an appointment may have been, they would scarcely have outweighed the objections that would have been apparent to anyone aware of the specially degraded position to which the Jews of Majorca had been reduced.

The fanaticism and extreme cruelty with which the Jews were for so long persecuted is perhaps the one serious stain in the island's record. Their sufferings in Spain were, if possible, mild in comparison with what they suffered in Majorca and whereas in Spain the feeling against them was not by any means unanimously hostile, in Majorca the utter execration in which they were held seems to have been universal. Even three and a half centuries after the height of the persecution and the forcible conversion of those who escaped execution, we are told by a distinguished Majorcan historian that the most popular book among all classes of Majorcans was Father Francisco Garau's "La Fe Triunfante", in which the author recounts in revolting detail the agonies of the Jews who suffered in the *auto da fe* of 1691. Señor Oliver refers to one passage in which Father Garau describes the burning of one Jorge Aguilo. "He stood like a statue. When the flames reached him he fought them off and tried to shield himself, and so resisted until he could bear no more. He was as fat as a sucking pig, and being on fire inside, his flesh being consumed like burning wood, his entrails fell out in the middle, like a Judas." "If," writes Oliver, Father Garau delights in this spectacle, it is because the whole people delight in it also. This work is a reflection, an emanation of the spirit of the masses..."

Small wonder then, that a descendant of one of Jorge Aguilo's fellow sufferers, who was another British Vice-Consul during the closing years of the XVIIIth century and the first two decades of the XIXth, should not have been received as Sir John Carr complained, in respectable Majorcan circles. Not only was he not received but no Majorcan Gentile would even so much as deign to speak to him and it was considered magnanimous of the Captain

General to permit him to send presents of fruit and game for the viceregal table.

The Chuetas, i.e. Judias, "Jew-boys"* as the local Jews are called, were objects of derision as well as hatred and this same unfortunate British Vice Consul was the victim of a well-known and frequently repeated story illustrating this. In the Convent of the Dominicans at Palma, the headquarters of the Inquisition, whose ruins inspired George Sand with some reflections strikingly similar to those which Charles Dickens recorded after his visit to the Palace of the Popes at Avignon, there were kept portraits of many of those Jews, who had been burnt at the stake. Among them was an ancestor of the British Vice-Consul who, hoping no doubt to efface at least one trace of his unhappy origins, asked the monks to let him have the portrait. They gave it him to his great happiness, but let it be known soon afterwards that they had kept a copy.

Sir John Carr, who was warned on arrival at Palma of the Consul's precarious social position, thought it prudent to decline his invitation to stay at the Consulate. Sir John was not the sort of man to incur the displeasure of polite society and possibly even total ostracism by flouting convention for the sake of racial and religious tolerance. Yet he had the generosity or the guile to give credit to another, who dared to do that from which he himself had shrunk. He tells his readers that "The Hon. Frederick North during his stay at Palma, resided at the house of the consul, for the purpose of softening the absurd, but bitter prejudices the people had against him, but neither the talents, learning, unparallelled suavity of temper and manners, nor rank of his distinguished guest could effect any change in the public mind." I have not been able to discover when this noble and lovable eccentric visited Majorca, but if he was then already "distinguished", I imagine the visit must have taken place either when he was Secretary of State for Corsica, or on his way back from being first Governor of Ceylon or finally and most probably when he was travelling to Corfu in 1809 and just before Carr landed at Palma.

It is hardly surprising that North should have failed to reform the citizens of Palma. Though they no doubt respected him and possibly may have liked him, they may be excused if they found it difficult to take too seriously the opinions of Byron's "illustrious humbug" and Creevey's "ramshackle fellow", whose disregard for conventional dress may well have been displayed in Palma. Had he not once, years before, turned up at the British Enbassy at Aranjuez in the dress of a Spanish mule driver? Yet all or almost all who knew him, spoke of his charm of manner. Paoli found him "easy of access", the Queen of the Two Sicilies loved to pass the time of day with him; Lord Holland "liked him extremely" because "his manner is so peculiar and his conversation so agreeable" and Charles Burney was never happier than when he came to visit him at Chelsea Hospital "since his pleasant wit, practical urbanity and persevering love of enterprise made him full of original entertainment." William Beckford of Fonthill alone among his acquaintance seems to have disliked him; "a jaundiced shambling figure" (he was often crippled with the gout) he calls him, and what was worse, adds that he was reckoned by the young ladies of the English colony at Lisbon to be a "nasty man".

---

*According to Alexander Laborde, *Chueta* is derived from the French word *Chouette* meaning a "Screech Owl". I was saved from repeating this howler (!) by Mr Robert Graves, who pointed out to me the correct derivation.

He was undeniably and even excessively eccentric and his eccentricity increased with age. Even as a very young man when he was putting Mr Gibbon "in good humour with his islands of Ithaca and Corfu" the observant Maria Holroyd found him "charming, though a wonderful oddity." In Corfu, the favourite in his trio of islands, he used to "go about dressed up like Plato with a gold band round his mad pate and flowing drapery of a purple hue." Sir Charles Napier, himself no stuffed shirt, thought him "a queer fish" but "very pleasant, addressing every person in a different language and always in that which the person addressed did not understand." Clearly De Quincey's "semi-delirious lord" was not the sort of person to make a serious impression on the strait-laced conservative admirers of the Abbe Garau.

Though Majorca never became a British colony like her lesser sister Minorca, she did, like most Mediterranean islands at one or more periods in their history, experience a British military occupation. During the War of the Spanish Succession the preponderance of British naval power in the Mediterranean made it possible for the Allies to win the Balearic Islands for the Archduke Charles or King Charles III, as he was then referred to by the supporters of his candidature for the Spanish throne. The islands were held at the beginning of hostilities by the partisans of the rival claimant, the Duke of Anjou and there were French garrisons in both Majorca and Minorca. The Archduke was however confident that the inhabitants were "well affected" to him and at the end of August 1706 it was decided that Admiral Sir John Leake, who commanded the British Squadron in the Mediterranean should attempt the reduction of Iviza and Majorca, but not Minorca. Iviza declared for the Archduke on September 8th immediately on the arrival of the fleet, which five days later, appeared off Palma.

The Admiral had hoped that Majorca would also "declare upon sight of the fleet, without any trouble", but he was to be disappointed. The Viceroy was strongly attached to the Bourbon interest and this attachment was rendered the more secure by the presence at Palma of the French garrison. Accordingly, on being summoned to surrender he returned a reply to the effect that Palma would be defended to the last extremity. A second summons was similarly dismissed, whereupon doubts began to be raised among certain officers of the fleet, notably Sir George Byng, about the feasibility of taking the place. Admiral Leake did not agree with these faint hearted views as well "from the general good inclination the inhabitants bore to King Charles as from the effect a few shells and some shot might have upon a people unacquainted with such things." The Admiral turned out to be perfectly right, for several shots, though they fell short of the city, were enough to convince the inhabitants of the righteousness of the Archduke's cause and the wickedness of any who attempted to deny it. One of the Duke of Anjou's party was murdered and the Viceroy had to seek refuge in his palace, while some of the chief men of the island waited on the Admiral with a flag of truce and offers of capitulations. Hostages were exchanged, the English being Captain Wager, afterwards Admiral Sir Charles Wager and Captain George Acton.

On the 18th September, the Capitulations were agreed, by which the island was surrendered to King Charles III. The terms included guarantees for the safety of the Duke of Anjou's supporters, provision for the repatriation of the French garrison and safeguards for Church property. The Castle at Porto Pi was handed over to a small garrison of British marines and, to celebrate the new regime, the Admiral and his senior officers were given a gala entertainment by the new Viceroy at the Almudaina Palace. Sir John sailed away for England on September 23rd, his bloodless conquest of Majorca having been accomplished in less than a week.

The English garrison remained in Palma for the next two years but was replaced by an Italian regiment when Minorca was occupied. This operation was launched from the larger island which provided both guns and troops for General Stanhope's army. The General also discovered that there was "at Majorca a magazine of masts" - a century later Nelson valued Corsica as a source of masts - and Sir George Byng was instructed to get possession of them and take them to Port Mahon.

By the Treaty of Utrecht (1713), Majorca reverted to the Spanish Crown in the person of Philip V and the close political ties with which she had been bound to England were soon to be broken. But some of the islanders were loath to see the English connexion end and in 1714 Henry Neal, the Surveyor General for Minorca, reported that he had "intimations from Majorca that they would be very willing to obtain the protection of the English by an annual payment." Neal did not feel competent to give any advice on the matter and nothing seems to have been done about his "intimations".

However Majorca still held out for the Archduke and in June 1715 a Spanish fleet was sent to Palma to bring the island to heel. Had it not been for the timely intervention of the English squadron at Minorca, those Majorcans who had actively supported Charles and his allies would have received short shrift from their victorious opponents. Fortunately the British Admiral was not the kind of man who would stand by and leave his country's friends to their fate, while he sought permission from the Government to save them.

Lord Forbes, Third Earl of Granard, was a man of fabulous energy and, even in an age when super versions of the Renaissance man abounded, his attainments, talents and achievements are highly impressive. Soldier, sailor - he was at one moment at the head of a troop of horse at the next captain of a ship of the line - diplomatist, politician, economist, agriculturist, coloniser, colonial governor and family man, he was all these things and some of them simultaneously. (Cartographer too perhaps? The map in Colin Campbell's translation of Dameto and Mut was presented to the translator by Lord Forbes.) Small wonder that Sir Robert Walpole thought him "too busy and curious".

Having heard of the approach of the Spanish fleet with a strong force of French troops on board, Lord Forbes, who was a close friend of the Viceroy of Majorca, the Marquis de Rubi, decided on his own authority to take his small squadron to Palma to give what protection he could to the Imperialists, as the supporters of the Austrian Archduke were called. He arrived in fact in Palma Bay a day earlier than the Spanish squadron, whose Admiral became understandably highly incensed at what he must have regarded as Forbes's totally unwarranted interference. His lordship having failed to obtain what he considered to be reasonable capitulation terms for his friends, incited them to take vigorous action to resist the French besiegers. He advocated and planned scorched earth measures and these were duly put into effect, with the result that the French felt obliged to moderate their demands. Finally, after the exercise of a good deal of bluff and several strained interviews with the Spanish Admiral, Forbes was successful in reaching a satisfactory settlement and departed for Port Mahon, taking with him the Marquis de Rubi and his German troops.

After this experience, relations between British Minorca and Spanish Majorca seem to have sadly deteriorated, each island being represented in the other almost exclusively by each other's undesirables. Majorca became a sanctuary for murderers and deserters from Minorca, and Minorca offered mischievous refuge for smugglers from Majorca. The Governor and the Captain General bombarded each other with requests for extradition but without effect. The Majorcans, who have a horror of capital punishment (except perhaps where Jews were concerned?) and who are seldom - as a result? - guilty of crimes of violence, had no intention of handing over to the un-tender mercies of British justice fellow Balearicites, and the British retaliated by giving sympathetic shelter and quite possibly encouragement to people wanted by the Spanish customs.

Another source of irritation to both was the ecclesiastical jurisdiction claimed by the Bishop of Majorca over Minorca, which had always formed a part of his diocese. The British authorities, who had appropriated the church revenues of Minorca to the Crown, found it less easy to destroy the Bishop's influence, which they feared would be subversive to the colony. The clergy in Minorca for their part continued to acknowledge his authority and vigorously resisted attempts to make them deny it. The Bishop, though deprived of his revenues, was not entirely dependent on spiritual weapons in his feud with the British. He still retained the right to appoint parish priests in Minorca, one of whom, a native of Buñola, was his staunchest champion. All this caused much annoyance to at least one governor of the colony.

British suspicion of Majorca was due in large measure to ignorance about the island, ignorance which was only slightly dispelled by the publication in 1716 of an English translation of Dameto and Mut's "History of the Balearic Islands". The translator, one Colin Campbell who was an officer serving with the Minorca garrison considered that "the larger Isle, which makes the chief Subject of the following work, ought at present to be better known to his British Majesty's Subjects than it has been hitherto."

Campbell was probably echoing the opinions of his superior officers, who would have felt more secure if they had known what was going on at Palma. They required not only general information about Majorca but regular reports on local activity and particularly on any that concerned the colony. The question was who should provide these reports. Vice-Consul Cortes had apparently had no successor and in the 1720's the Governor of Minorca was urging on the home Government the need to appoint an English consul in Majorca "it being a great service and safety to the island of Minorca". The Government objected that British trade with Majorca was not enough to support a consul, whereupon Governor Carpenter suggested that he might be paid out of the ecclesiastical revenues of Minorca. The Treasury was delighted with this proposal and in 1731 Samuel Scott was appointed Consul at Palma at a salary of £150 per annum payable from moneys that had formerly belonged to the Bishop of Majorca.

Though Anglo-Majorcan trade may not have been sufficient alone to justify a consul at Palma, it was not entirely negligible. Possibly due to the Minorcan garrison, a number of Majorcan products were introduced during the XVIIIth century to the British public. In those days the gentlemen of England drank, among other things, Majorcan wines and Majorcan spirits. The white wine, known as Albaflor, which comes from Bañalbufar, was especially appreciated and is now reckoned by M. Andre Simon to be the best Majorcan white wine.

Much of the wine from the vineyards of Bañalbufar was used to distill acqua vita. The product of the Felanitx distilleries was said to be the best in Europe and was exported to many countries including England.

Samuel Scott remained Consul at Majorca until his death and was succeeded by Abraham Whitham, who also came from Minorca where he had long been resident. During the operations that led to the recapture of Minorca from the Spanish in 1763, he rendered signal service as an overseer of workmen, rather like the manager of the Formentor Hotel, one imagines. The military were so pleased with him that he was appointed an engineer "to encourage him and give better pay". When the operations were over he was recommended to the Duke of Marlborough, who intended to reward him with a civilian job, as he had no qualifications as an engineer. However the Duke died before anything had been arranged and Whitham and his large family remained unprovided for. So when the post of consul in Majorca fell vacant, he was appointed and the £150 a year from the Bishop's revenues was appropriated for his salary.

It looked as if an anxious paterfamilias was in sight of a steady income, when a serious hitch occurred. The Spaniards, having heard of his exploits during the reconquest of Minorca, refused to have a military man as consul. The Minorca Government persisted however in their efforts to reward Whitham and secured a certificate from the Master General of the Ordinance in London that their protege had never been commissioned as an engineer. This document evidently had the desired effect, for Abraham Whitham was at last able to take up his post in 1766, three years after having been appointed.

When he lived in Minorca, the new Consul had been on friendly terms with the officers of the garrison and he took care to keep in touch after he had moved to Palma. He was amply repaid for his trouble when one of his many children made the best match in the Balearics, and the ex-overseer's daughter became the Governor's lady. Anne Whitham's marriage to Major General the Hon. James Murray took place shortly before that veteran of the siege of Quebec was himself forced to surrender to the French in Minorca. Not that Anne suffered the rigours of a siege for her husband packed her off in good time to the safety of Leghorn.

Murray, popularly known as "Old Minorca", numbered literary men among his acquaintance, to whom he may have been introduced by his elder brother, Dr Johnson's friend, Lord Elibank. One of these acquaintances was the agriculturalist Arthur Young, author of the celebrated "Tours", who after a rapid and rather unsatisfactory excursion into Catalonia in 1787, contributed to his "Annals of Agriculture" some notes on Majorca. In these he reported that the climate of Majorca was the "most delicious" that had been experienced by various persons well acquainted with France, Italy, Spain and Portugal, "that the island might be made a paradise" and that it was one of the cheapest spots in Europe to live in.

According to Young, "men of the better sort live comfortably and bring up a family on £150 a year sterling." Young's information was derived partly from letters he had received from General Murray when Governor of Minorca. No doubt the item about "men of the better sort" was a contribution by the General, who must have been well aware of his father-in-law the Consul's salary. After all, in him there was a striking instance of a gentleman who had brought up a family triumphantly on £150 a year sterling.

Another military correspodent, writing home about the same time as the

Governor, had acquired some information possibly from Mrs Murray. Ensign John Moore, the future hero of Corunna had heard that "the climate of Minorca was not nearly so equable as that of Majorca."

The Peninsular War, while it delayed Majorca's development as a warm weather refuge for British expatriates, must have helped considerably to propagate its attractions. Many a British sailor and soldier, who went ashore at Palma and was hospitably received, assuredly passed the word round that it would make a delightful place for honourable retirement. Before the War ended, Majorca just missed an almost certain chance of world wide publicity. In 1813 Edward Harley, Earl of Oxford visited the island with his wife. Byron was to have accompanied them on the Mediterranean tour but, having tired of his liaison with Lady Oxford, he contented himself with seeing them off at Portsmouth. A pity, for Childe Harold would have found Valldemosa worth a stanza.

It was still the exception rather than the rule for English Mediterranean travellers to include Majorca in their itineraries and the island seldom figures in their travel diaries. Chopin wrote in a letter in December 1838 that there was not a single Englishman in the island - not even a consul. The Consulate at Palma, after a brief period of activity during the last years of the Peninsular War, had reverted to its former state of somnolence. The "career" consul, who had been appointed to deal with prize money claims was replaced by an honorary local resident, whose official duties were evidently not exacting. Mr Christmas reported with disapproval in 1850 that the Consul was absent from his post for five days without anyone having been put in charge while he was away.

Nevertheless contact with the United Kingdom was slowly becoming more frequent. With the removal of some of the worst restrictions on the Majorcan economy under the comparatively enlightened rule of Queen Maria Cristina and her chief minister Mendizabal - once Bauza's fellow exile in London, the friend of George Sand, the hero of a celebrated interview with George Borrow and of another with Disraeli's Sidonia, who beheld in him "one like myself, the son of a Nuevo Cristiano, a Jew of Arragon" - the island's foreign trade began to revive and especially with the United Kingdom. The 1830's saw the first imports of English coal and the construction by English engineers of the Palma gas works. The first steamship to ply between Barcelona and Palma was brought out from England and operated by Scotch engineers. A paddle wheeler with a funnel like an elongated chef's cap, it was called "El Mallorquin" and had the distinction of bringing Chopin and George Sand to Majorca. It was followed by seven more vessels and by 1870 regular services were being provided by them between Majorca and Barcelona and Majorca and Valencia. At the same time the export to England of Soller oranges was greatly expanded and it is probably due to this trade that Soller has developed a particularly close association with the English.

Trade with the United Kingdom was stimulated by the operations of the Majorca Land Company in the Albufera and in 1872 it received a further impetus when the Majorca Railway Company was formed, the capital for which was subscribed entirely by local investors. The materials for the construction of the railway, the locomotives and the rolling stock were purchased from Nasmyth Wilson and Co. of Manchester and Brown Marshall & Co. of Birmingham and were imported direct to Palma in seven British vessels and one Spanish. The construction of the railway was carried out entirely by Majorcan engineers and architects at a cost of £3,000 per kilometre. The journey to Inca, when the railway was opened in 1875 took 64 minutes and the first class single fare was 1/6 and the second class 1/-. Eighty years later the same journey took exactly one minute less but the fares had gone up to 3/3 and 2/3.

Obviously the directors of the Majorca Railway Company had not thought it necessary to plough back much of their profits by renewing their capital equipment. I was glad of this for, by failing to do so, they had preserved for our enjoyment a delightful antique and the possibility of a sentimental flight into the Majorca of eighty years previously when the Archduke Luis Salvator, with the spell of the Greater Aphrodisiad upon him, was making love to a peasant girl of Miramar, and when Mr Consul Bidwell was scrutinising closely the courting procedure of the Majorcan male.

One sultry afternoon we repaired to the Majorca Railway Station at Palma, an untidy little open-air terminus whose platform was thronged with people. The afternoon train for Inca was about to leave with as much hurried emotion as precedes the departure of a *Grand Express Europeen*. It did not matter that the distance was a few miles and that the engine and carriages looked as if they dated from the inauguration of the railway. Clearly the Majorcans enjoyed it as much as they did on that first memorable day when the whole of the island assembled to speed the first train on its way. We got into a second class compartment, but, finding it too crowded, transferred to a first, which was occupied by two sleepy Majorcan gentlemen. After a great deal of violent whistling and other station noises, the train groaned into life with a succession of back-breaking jolts and we began to bump slowly along the rusty grass-grown track. A fly buzzed distractedly about the compartment as the Majorcan gentlemen dozed unmindful of it. Immense smuts, enormous soot flakes blew in at the window and softly smudged our faces and the immaculate antimacassars. The guard blew in too and softly punched our tickets. There was no corridor so he walked along the footboard, which the slowness of the train enabled him to do in perfect safety. We stopped for a long time at Santa Maria, where our somnolent fellow passengers got out with the fly. There was some delay at this station, while important shuntings took place, then heralded by a tremendous brouhaha from the platform the train lurched with a portentous shudder - into reverse. We arrived eventually at Inca, feeling rather dead, but dead on time.

The 1870's saw a further and almost literal connexion with England when the first submarine cable between Majorca and the Spanish mainland was laid. It was supplied by W.T. Henley of Woolwich in 1878 but, owing to the sea bed being twice as deep as marked on the charts, was found to be too short. It had to be returned to England for overhaul and lengthening and was successfully laid the following year.

In spite of the increased trade, the English gasworks, the English steamers, the English railway, and the English cable, not to mention the Land Company, Majorca remained virtually a closed book to the English continental tourist. There were not indeed many books to open about it. There were translations of two French works, Alexander de Laborde's "A View of Spain" and Grasset de St Sauveur's "Travels through the Balearic and Pithiusan Islands between 1801 and 1805", both of which appeared just before the publication of Sir John Carr's book, but of whose existence he seems to have been unaware. Nothing further appears to have been written in English about Majorca for another forty years.

In 1850 a Church of England clergyman, the Rev. Henry Christmas, was touring the "Shores and Islands of the Mediterranean" with "a dear and valued friend" and an account of their peregrinations was published the following year in three volumes, one of which was devoted entirely to Majorca and Minorca. Christmas was an observant traveller and a firm believer in doing in Rome what Romans do. Indeed he carried this principle to extremes if he followed the advice he gave to his readers, "The costume of the country is always the best to wear: a beard and a moustache are great advantages and the less luggage the better." English visitors to the island were scarce, he reported, though those that did come were well received and indeed popular on account of the useful assistance given by the British in expelling the French, which was much appreciated.

One of these rare visitors was William Dodd, who spent "Three Weeks in Majorca" in 1862 and another was an English gentleman evidently of somewhat advanced tastes, who at about the same time travelled around the island with his young wife, two children and a tent. In 1874 Bidwell declared that so few British visited the island that it might as well be in the Pacific as in the Mediterranean, and C.W. Wood, whose "Letters from Majorca" appeared twelve years later, confirmed this. He complained that it was so seldom visited that he was unable to obtain any help from Thomas Cook and Son in arranging his journey, for they had no information about Majorca.

The continuing neglect by the English tourist of an island whose loveliness had received unqualified eulogies in every account of it that had hitherto appeared may be explained in part by the reluctance of most people to embark on a second sea crossing after having once put behind them the terrors of the Channel, and in part to the inadequacy of Majorcan hotels. Bidwell for example, deplored the fact that there was "not a decent inn in the capital" and O'Shea in his "Guide to Spain" (1889) says discouragingly that of the inns at Palma "the least bad is Fonda de Mallorca; then come Fonda del Vapor etc."

If there were no hotels of a standard of luxury sufficiently high to attract the fastidious tourist, the inns, with which the natives were content, were probably as good as the best among equivalent establishments in any part of Europe. Christmas says that what he saw of them was "greatly to their advantage in point of cleanliness, civility and reasonable charges" and at the boarding house where he stayed at Palma for 22/- a week (full pension) everything was scrupulously clean. O'Shea too, echoing Christmas, concedes that "There are, tolerably good inns, hostels where civility, cleanliness, good will and moderate charge make up for other wants."

The few English people who did come to Majorca in the eighties and nineties of the last century - the British Colony numbered thirty-nine in 1875 - seem generally to have taken furnished houses, the fashion having been set by the Marquis of Bute, who rented for some years the mansion of Bendinat beyond El Terreno. This Majorcan Strawberry Hill was erected by a descendant of the Marquis de la Romana near the place where, according to the legend, Jaime the Conqueror, having eaten after his victory over the Moors, remarked that he had dined well.

Lord Bute's influence on the development of Majorca as a favourite resort of the English was probably less than that of another visitor to the island in the '80s. This was Oscar Browning, who spent the Easter holidays of 1881 at Palma with a pupil named Paul Bevan. Browning was an Eton master, an historian and a terrific snob, who counted among his friends a large number of crowns and coronets and from the dizzy social eminence to which he had climbed felt able to regard with something verging on patronage his much more famous namesake and distant kinsman Robert.

Browning and his young companion enjoyed their stay at Palma, where they horrified the locals by bathing every morning at six. In those days Majorcans thought it unwise to enter the water before Midsummer's Day and even then we can be sure they would not have ventured in before breakfast. They expected, Browning relates, that he and his friend would fall down dead on their way back from the beach. Their expectations were in some measure fulfilled, for Paul Bevan was cut off in the flower of his youth a year or two after his Majorcan holiday.

The effect on the schoolmasters of England must have been considerable when the news got around that the great Oscar had spent a "vac" in Majorca. From then on the island's future as a haunt of the English holidaymaking classes was assured.

As the nineteenth century drew to a close and women's emancipation began to spread, Oscar Browning's pioneering in Majorca was reinforced by the unrecorded efforts of members of a sister profession. These were made possible, appropriately enough, by the personality of Queen Victoria, which made itself felt even in the Greater Aphrodisiad. I have been told that her portrait used to be displayed not only in many a Palma shopwindow, no doubt partly for commercial reasons, but that it was also to be seen in private houses. So powerfully were the Majorcan nobility impressed by the moral reputation both of the Great Queen and her subjects that they began to entrust the care and education of their daughters to young English gentlewomen. These governesses received every consideration from their Majorcan employers and were regarded as members of the family rather than as employees. This sort of treatment, to which they were not always accustomed in their own country, must have made Majorca appear particularly idyllic to them, and it is not hard to imagine what long and detailed accounts must have flowed homewards from their glowing pens, increasing the island's fame among a section of the British public that was becoming more and more tourist conscious.

During the decade preceding the first World War English people in steadily increasing numbers visited Palma and for their spiritual convenience the Church of England service was read every Sunday morning by a Wesleyan minister in a mission room in the suburb of Santa Catalina. Among these visitors though not, it may safely be said, among the congregation at the mission room, were Hilaire Belloc in 1906 and Havelock Ellis two years later. They were the vanguard of legions of literary persons who were later to invade the island. The first luxury hotel, the "Grand Hotel" was built in 1904 to accommodate the growing number of tourists and the distinguished Spanish author, Azorín, who stayed there in 1906, described it with enthusiasm and studied naivete. "We arrive in front of a wonderful new building: the carriage stops and we get out. We enter the hotel. I have seen nothing like it in Spain, not even the Cristina at Algeciras. It is a vast hotel in the English style with a spacious marble entrance hall, with little tables and rocking chairs, a high roof, clean, glistening. I feel I am in the Grosvenor Hotel in London, of such sweet memories. 'This is beautiful,' I say to Albareda (the Manager). A. bows and smiles ... We go into the dining room. It is decorated simply and elegantly; on one side there are two paintings by Mir, (a well known Catalan painter), large and fantastic; Rusiñol (the famous Majorcan painter) has painted for the other wall three of his subtle and romantic visions. This dining room is for winter use; when there is a large influx of tourists in summer, they use a smaller room..." I could not find the Grand Hotel and it was only after leaving Majorca that I learned that it had been so badly damaged by Italian bombs during the Civil War, that the owners could not afford to repair it. They sold it to the government to house the Pensions Ministry.

Though Cooks were apparently still unknown in Majorca, it soon became clear to others that there would be scope for more than one luxury hotel at Palma and the portentous front door of the "Victoria" first began to revolve only three years after the "Grand" was opened. In the same year Margaret D'Esté's "With a Camera in Majorca" was published, the first book in English on the Balearic Islands of many by women writers. Miss Bellingham's "Ups and Downs of Spanish Travel", written in 1883 "at the suggestion of a few friends" is not exclusively about Majorca or the Balearics but she deserves an honourable place among lady pioneers. She and her female companions caused consternation among the Majorcans, because they travelled without a male escort. Here at last was proof that George Sand's prophecy that "a time will doubtless come when delicate amateurs and even pretty women will be able to go to Palma without any more fatigue and discomfort than going to Geneva" had been fulfilled and, if a member of the fair sex could go to Majorca and survive and write a book about it, then the hazards could not be so very great. So must many a wavering Edwardian male have argued to himself and it has been authoritatively stated that Mrs Boyd's "The Fortunate Isles" which appeared four years later, was a major factor in popularising Majorca as a tourist resort.

By the late twenties the "Greater Aphrodisiad" had become a recognised haven for the intelligentsia, and poets and artists, dons and housemasters were flocking to its still uncrowded shores. There were more visits by famous literary figures. Hilaire Belloc was back again in 1926 and D.H. Lawrence came three years later, when he had only ten months more to live. He was already sickening for his last illness and, perhaps because of this, didn't really care for Majorca. He liked his hotel, the Principe Alfonso, but found both the food and the bill excessive. He liked the sea and the flowers and Palma itself "all a funny heapy-heap of buff and white", but the wind that blows sometimes quite sharply in April bothered him. Then he had bouts of malaria and people got on his nerves. Though it was undeniably lovely "so fresh and calm and sunny", yet there was a certain something about the atmosphere " a human deadness and a foolish intellectual sort of resistance to life", which bored him and made him not want to stay. The Lawrences spent a weekend at Cala Ratjada in the north easternmost corner of the island beyond Arta. Though it was brilliant and sunny the wind caught at his chest and spoilt it for him. When their stay was almost at an end, his opinion of the island seems to have changed little.He described an afternoon, which in spite of mortal sickness he almost enjoyed. "It is really rather lovely here, warm and sunny and blue, and so remote, if one goes a bit away. Of course we know a number of residents - come to lunch kind of thing - but nice. Today we motored along the coast to a lonely bay with pine trees down to the sea, and the Mallorquin servants cooked Spanish rice over a fire in a huge pot, and the others bathed, and I sat under a tree like the ancient of days and drank small beer -microscopic bock - and it was really very lovely, no one in the world but us. This is a wonderful place for doing nothing -the time passes rapidly in a long stretch of nothingness - broken by someone fetching us out in a motor or somebody else in a donkey-cart. It is very good for my health I believe. This letter is my most serious contribution to literature these six weeks. There's something I like about the island - but the people are dullish."

Lawrence did not name any of the permanent "come to lunch sort of thing" residents he saw. They might have included Robert Graves, who had settled in the island the year before the Lawrences' visit. By then Majorca had become a haven of peace for many such as he; who sought a country and a climate which would benefit both their health and their pocket. Some account of them is given in the next chapter.

## CHAPTER IX
## ROBERT GRAVES AND OTHER RESIDENTS

Soon after the First World War, the British colony in Majorca had grown so far as to make possible the formation of a British Association. It was run from a library and tea room at No37 Calle Catorce de Abril which became Avenida Calvo Sotelo and is now Avinguda Joan Miro. This is one of the principal streets of El Terreno, the former aristocratic quarter of Palma. It was also the resort of British and American expatriates since the days when Uncle Lee La Trobe Bateman had his beautiful house there in the 1880s. So strong was the effect of their presence on the neighbourhood that when José Maria Salaverria was staying in an hotel there in 1933, he had some difficulty in convincing himself that he was in a Spanish country or even in Southern Europe. Sometimes he thought he might be in a South American town and at others in an Anglo-Saxon village. On leaving his hotel he saw in front of him "a library fixed up in a sort of garage; if I ask for a Spanish daily, the attendant excuses himself; he only has English magazines, novels and newspapers. Next to the LIBRERY [sic] there is a bar; everyone in it of both sexes is Anglo-Saxon. And that man with a pipe in his mouth is a Yankee; another is English... And the natives? There are moments when I wonder whether they exist."

The library was the creation of an electronics engineer, F. G. Short who had come to Spain at the invitation of the Spanish government to erect Marconi wireless stations in various parts of the mainland and finally at Puerto Soller in Majorca. While engaged on this task it occurred to him that there was scope for a business to provide services for the P & O liners that regularly called at Palma. It was from what the mystified author of "Viaje a Mallorca" thought was some sort of garage that Short launched the taxis and buses he hired to the P & O or their passengers for tours of the island. In this way many an Anglo-Indian was introduced to the island's charms and perhaps tempted to return later and even stay for good.

The sort of garage had been the guardhouse of a building that was believed to have been the summer residence of Queen Isabella and it was there that, after the tea tables and chairs had been moved to one side, tea dances used to take place. In 1925, the British Association, which F. G. Short helped to found, invited the Reverend James Johnson, Chaplain of St George's, Barcelona, and Head of the Mediterranean Mission to Seamen to take services at the library, where the chairs were once more rearranged for the purpose. Two years later the association rented a subterranean part of Queen Isabella's villa, which had been used as a soda-water bottling factory, and in 1934 it became the first Anglican Church in Majorca.

As a place of worship it had its drawbacks. The officiating Minister, who before the appointment of a Chaplain, still came from Barcelona, had to contend with noises off either from a lavatory being flushed from above or from a cockerel crowing on a window-sill. The latter interruption was doubtless less frequent than in the magnificent Cathedral of Santo Domingo de la Calzada where a cockerel in its painted cage regularly crows at Mass (see Ford for the authorising legend). Until 1968 when a law was passed giving religious freedom in Spain, the Church had to put up with restrictions imposed by the local authorities and often the presence of armed guardias civiles during the services. Despite all this the Church was always filled to overflowing.

On the outbreak of the Spanish Civil War in July 1936 the Church was filled to overflowing not with the faithful but with their furniture. The British residents were evacuated in HMS Grenville and all their possessions, except what they could carry in a hold-all, were stacked in the church which was filled to the roof.

Shortly after the British Association had started to rent the ex-soda water bottle factory the island was visited by one who helped to swell its numbers and in due course transform it into the British-America Club. Sir Harry Brittain described in his autobiography, "Happy Pilgrimage", his visit to Majorca in the winter of 1927/28 and what prompted it. He was having lunch with the Spanish ambassador in London, the Marquis Merry del Val when he complained about the awfulness of the weather. The Marquis, having established that Brittain's knowledge of Majorca was limited to a few hours call at Palma, doubtless in a P & O liner, suggested he should go for a winter holiday there. Brittain took his advice at once and a connoisseur of good holidays had one of the best. He and his wife fell in love with the island and its delightful people, as he was happy to tell the Editor of El Dia. He also received a call from the Governor who, having no doubt been tipped off by the Embassy in London, asked him to write an article on his visit for an English paper. This he promised to do and in February 1929 the Windsor Magazine, which was comparable with the Strand but which has no equivalent today, published an article on "Majorca where the sun shines" by Sir Harry Brittain, KBE, CMG, M.P., "an old and seasoned traveller", who had "come across what is to him a new and hitherto unsuspected paradise on earth". Praise such as this from such a source was music to the ears of the Spanish tourist authorities. Having obtained the permission of author and publisher, they printed a large number of copies of the article in two or three languages which were distributed all over the world. The result was that Brittain was for years bombarded with scores of requests for information and advice on the island including one on its suitability for an Anglo-Indian's retirement.

Sir Harry's advice would have been taken very seriously indeed by future residents such as Cecil Aldin who knew of his visit, for he was an immensely important and influential person. A glance at his entry in a book of reference demonstrates that this was so. He was, for example, a Director of daily and weekly newspapers and other companies, a broadcaster "Home and Overseas", Founder and Vice-President of the Pilgrims, a Vice-President of the Royal Commonwealth Society, a member of the Committee of the English Speaking Union, the originator of the first Imperial Press Conference, Founder of the Commonwealth Press Union, Director of Intelligence Ministry of National Service during the First World War and a long serving MP. A mighty sportsman of international renown, he was also one of the founders and most active members of the Anti-Socialist Union. This last achievement which obliged his namesake, Vera, to assure the reader of her "Testament" that she was no relation, would have been reassuring to many a pensioner contemplating retirement in Majorca. They could rely on him when he wrote of the "many opportunities for social foregathering – a pleasant British Colony of charming and hospitable folk" not to mention "the most helpful of British Vice-Consuls". He was equally enthusiastic about the roads, the grottos of Drachs and Arta, the view of Palma from his hotel at El Terreno, the excellence of the cuisine and the reliability of the bills. He did admit there was no golf course, a disadvantage that was later remedied.

What impressed him most was the wonderful climate which enabled him in mid-winter to bathe in the sea most days. He had been assured both by his "old friend, Frederick Chamberlin, the American writer, who is responsible for more than one delightful and useful book on the island", and by an English General, who had served in many countries, that the climate was unsurpassed in the world. The English General sounds suspiciously like Brigadier General William Beckett, for whom his wife had written at his request a book "Free from War and Free from Sex" on their life at Soller (chapter IV). It was published in 1947 in the year of her death at well over 80 and nine years before his at the age of 98. Perhaps their longevity was in part due to the Majorcan climate.

Brittain's "most helpful of British Vice-Consuls" was Ivan Lake who had been appointed to this unsalaried post in 1924 at the age of 36. He resigned in November 1932 and was immediately succeeded by a different type of British Vice-Consul, to whose career as revealed in works of reference an element of mystery attaches. The Foreign Office List of 1933 recorded him as Lt.Commander A. Hillgarth RN. In 1938 the List showed him as Lt.Commander Alan Hillgarth OBE RN (Retd). He had been made OBE in May 1937 and given simultaneously the rank of Consul. The 1940 List recorded his resignation from the post of Consul at Palma and his appointment immediately after in August 1939 as Assistant Naval Attaché in Spain. In January 1943 he was made CMG and in October the same year his appointment in Spain, by then as Naval Attaché, was terminated. To have been made OBE and CMG in four years suggests that his services were outstanding and yet a Naval Officer of such distinction appears only once in the Navy Lists of the period. The List for July 1934 gives him as Lt.Commander Alan Hugh Hillgarth who on retirement commuted his pay. His promotion to Lt.Commander was dated 15 December 1927 but there is no trace of him either under Hillgarth or his previous name, Evans, in the Lists for 1928 or subsequent years. What could be the explanation for this apparently deliberate omission?

The likely answer is that Hillgarth was appointed to Palma not just to carry out normal consular functions such as marrying British subjects and coping with drunk ones. Might not his main task have been concerned with what in the eyes of some Officers and Gentlemen was the ungentlemanly business of secret intelligence? By the time of his appointment to Palma Mussolini's aggressive behaviour was causing alarm and later in September 1937 Churchill was writing to Eden about "the continual fortification of the Mediterranean by Italy against us" and the need for Anglo-French Naval cooperation "to prevent trouble arising out of the Balearics". In Madrid Hillgarth was certainly concerned with intelligence operations as was revealed by J. G. Beevor both in his book, "S.O.E. – Recollections and Reflections", and in a tribute to him in The Times after his death in February 1978. In his book he wrote that Hillgarth supervised secret activities in Spain on behalf of the ambassador, Sir Samuel Hoare, from whose "Ambassador on Special Mission" he quoted: "Captain Hillgarth, the embodiment of drive, was a veritable sleuth on the track of enemy submarines in Spanish waters. He also gave us valuable contacts that effectively helped at critical moments". Prominent among these, Beevor wrote in The Times, "but always in secrecy, was Don Juan March who...rendered services to the Allied cause unsurpassed in any neutral country". Hillgarth ended the war with a new wife and as Chief of Intelligence Staff Eastern Fleet and Chief of British Naval Intelligence Eastern Theatre.

However secret some of Hillgarth's duties may have been during his time in Majorca, his first wife's voluntary work needed no cover. A daughter of the first and last Baron Burghclere and the former wife of the Hon. Geoffrey Hope-Morley, afterwards Baron Hollenden, she married Hillgarth in 1929 after he had changed his name from Evans. In Majorca she became one of the leading supporters of the Anglican church in Palma. In the Foreword to Neville Waters' account of the church, the Bishop of Gibraltar mentioned her faithful devotion to it and Waters, who did more than any man to keep it alive, reckoned she did more than any woman. After the British residents were evacuated Mary Hillgarth "took it upon herself", he wrote, "to pay the rent on that first church [the old soda-water factory]...not only through the years of the Civil War, but on through the years of the Second World War" even though she was no longer married to the former Consul. Waters insisted that "if it had not been for her generous act it is almost certain that...the very right for the Anglican church to exist in Mallorca might have been jeopardised".

On 9 October 1966 the new church of St Philip and St James at Son Armadans, about three quarters of a mile from the old soda-water factory at El Terreno was consecrated. Named after the first Chaplain in Majorca, the Reverend Philip Coleman and the first to take services the Reverend James Johnson, it was built with money raised by members of the congregation. This included American residents between whom and the British there was much solidarity. Not only had the British Association become the British-American Club but Neville Waters organised annual American Thanksgiving dinners partly in aid of the building fund. At these dinners the American consul proposed "the Queen" and the British Consul proposed "the United States".

The Anglican Church in Palma had also become a focus not only of British and American solidarity but of good fellowship between Anglo-Saxon and their Majorcan hosts. It began when the church was designed by a Majorcan architect and built by local builders and local craftsmen and continued when the Bishop of Mallorca gave the Anglicans his help by making Roman Catholic churches outside Palma at Pollensa, Soller and other places both in Majorca and Minorca available for Anglican services. An even more remarkable indication that Majorcan fanaticism had greatly softened was provided in 1966, two years before the Religious Liberty Law was passed, when a Jewish Rabbi from Detroit held a Jewish service in the old soda-water factory church, the first such service to have been held in Majorca since the days of the Inquisition.

Exactly half a century before this event there was living in Majorca another American Jew who would not have attended the Rabbi's service. Gertrude Stein and her friend Alice Toklas, who were tired of the rigours of life in war-torn Paris and, being citizens of a still neutral country, were relatively free to travel, decided to seek peace and calm in Majorca which they had visited in the summer of 1913. They arrived at Palma in May 1915 and were so delighted with what they found that they rented a house in El Terreno and stayed for nearly a year. During that time Gertrude wrote some of her less obscure works. Among them were poems referring to her love affair with Alice which contained such lines as "Do you love me, sweetest, just as much as if I were English". She also excited the French Consul, who had been on Marshall Lyautey's staff in Morocco, with a piece of stale intelligence she had picked up in Tangier. In her confusingly entitled *The Autobiography of Alice B Toklas* she wrote that, when she and her friend were in Majorca, they and an American artist, William Cook, were the only Americans living in the island.

Whereas in 1932 when she wrote the book "a great many...seem to like it now". In 1916, according to her, "there were a few english [sic], about three families there". They included an old lady named Mrs Penfold, said to have been a descendant of one of Nelson's captains. Gertrude and Alice may have been having tea with her one day when an English boy of sixteen, Mark Gilbert, "with pacifist tendencies" was also present. The boy, like Gwendoline in the *Importance of Being Earnest*, refused cake, upon which Mrs Penfold told him that he was either old enough to fight for his country or young enough to eat cake. "Mark ate cake" wrote Gertrude.

Gertrude Stein's love of Majorca was the direct cause of Robert Graves becoming its most famous and among its longest staying English residents. In an article written in 1953 and reprinted in 1965 in his *Majorca Observed* he wrote that he went to live there on her recommendation. She had assured him that the Majorcans were "a cheerful clean and friendly people" and that if he "liked Paradise, Majorca was Paradise". And so in 1928 Robert Graves departed for Majorca where he built himself a house at Deyá. He had lived there happily for seven years when, on the outbreak of the Spanish Civil War, he received a note from the British Consul informing him that "this afternoon HMS Grenville will evacuate British residents; probably your last chance of leaving Spain in safety. Luggage limited to one hold-all". The note was addressed to "Dear Robert" and initialled "I.L." which suggests that Ivan Lake had been called in to assist in the evacuation of British subjects. Graves was strongly advised to take the opportunity and so he packed his manuscripts and some clothes into a hold-all and an hour later left with three friends in a taxi provided by the Consul. He had no time to deposit any of his possessions in the English church. In any case it would have been unnecessary for when he returned after ten years of dreary exile he found his house and garden untouched and he was greeted by his village friends with as many tears of welcome as they had shed on his departure.

Ann was a great admirer of Robert Graves's poetry and a friend of his daughter Jenny whom I had also met. It was on the strength of this and with the encouragement of Tomás Harris, who knew Robert and his new wife, that Ann introduced herself on the telephone and asked if we might call. She received a welcoming response and on 18 May 1955 we visited the Graves's at their flat in Guillermo Massot. After our return to England I sent an account of the visit which I had written for the first draft of this book to Graves for his approval. He wrote back to say that he did not "mind" it but suggested I should delete one reference as it might encourage "unwanted visitors". He reminded me that we came as friends of his daughter Jenny's "and all Jenny's friends are welcomed – if only because we so seldom see her ourselves". I had also recorded the visit in my diary and this account has, after forty years, at least the merit of immediacy which a more stylised version lacks. So though I cannot submit it now for his approval I hope he still would not "mind".

"Met Ann at Bar Figaro and we went together to call on Robert Graves at his flat. Found him most cordial, handsome, grey woolly hair, tall, dressed in blue jeans with a slit near the pocket. Wife told him he must change them but he said they were decent. 'Nice trousers don't you think?' He was in his work room with his elderly secretary. Windows shut: full of cigarette smoke. Gave us Fundadors. Told him about my proposed book. He was encouraging. Said that S.P.B. Mais was also planning a book on the island. Told me it had been visited by the Old Pretender but did not give more details. Told me of an incident in one of Marryat's novels that occurred in Majorca, when for a joke some ship's officers fired a gun to frighten a man reading by the sea and accidentally blew his head off". (The incident remembered by Graves, presumably from boyhood reading, is described in *Frank Mildmay* Chapter V). These scraps of information were imparted after I had told him that I wanted to investigate the island's connexion with what he called the "Englishry". He also developed his theory of George Sand's unhappiness during her stay in Majorca, which shortly afterwards formed the introduction to his translation of her *Voyage* (Chapter IV). Before we took our leave the Graves's said they might call on us on their tour of the island which they were about to begin. They were as good as their word and six days later they called at the Villa and spent much of the time playing with the children. They were delighted with the author of *Goodbye to All That* who carried the eldest on his shoulders down to the Formentor sands. He was evidently delighted not only with them but with their mother. Eighteen months later, when he wrote about the typescript of my book which he liked well enough to include some passages in an article on the Chuetas, he sent "best wishes to your wife, the beautiful ex-secret agent. We had a great time that day at Formentor!"

# SELECT BIBLIOGRAPHY

Dameto and Mut. *The Ancient and Modern History of the Balearic Islands*. London, 1716. Indispensable for anyone planning to write a book about Majorca.

Rev. H. Christmas, F.R.S. *The Shores and Islands of the Mediterranean*. London, 1851.

C. T. Bidwell, F.R.G.S. *The Balearic Islands*. London, 1876. The author, who was H.M. Consul at Palma, gives a lot of information of a consular kind not to be found elsewhere.

Gaston Vuillier. *The Forgotten Isles*. English translation, London, 1897.

Miguel S. Oliver. *Mallorca Durante la Primera Revolucion*. Palma, 1901. An absorbing account of the most interesting period of Majorca's history.

H. C. Shelley. *Majorca*. London, 1926. In spite of one colossal howler, the best general "guide" book in English.

Nina Larrey Duryea. *Mallorca the Magnificent*. London, 1927.

Gordon West. *Jogging Round Majorca*. London, 1929 (reprinted after being read on Radio 4 in 1994).

Bessie D. Beckett. *Memories of Majorca*. London, 1947.

Lady Shepherd. *Mediterranean Island*. London, 1949. A delightful account of Lady Shepherd's life in Majorca.

George Sand. *Un Hiver à Majorque*. Current edition by Calman-Levy. Biassed and inaccurate, but lively and readable. Also an annotated translation by Robert Graves, London, 1956.

Robert Graves. *Majorca Observed*. London, 1965.

To those who may not be satisfied with the above selection, I commend Thorwold Solberg's exhaustive bibliography, published by the Bibliographical Society of America.

According to O'Shea (*Guide to Spain*) a book called *Three Weeks in Majorca* by William Dodd, published by Chapman & Hall in 1863 at 3/- is worth reading. I have not been able to do this since in spite of the most exhaustive search I have not succeeded in tracing a copy.

# A NOTE ON THE ILLUSTRATIONS

"La literata Sand", as Rubén Darío somewhat contemptuously referred to her, says that she was stirred to write her celebrated account of "Un Hiver à Majorque" by a book that she found one morning lying on her table. This book was called "Souvenirs d'un Voyage d'Art a l'Ile de Majorque" and its author J. B. Laurens, whom George Sand condescendingly describes as "intelligent and laborious", should, also according to her, be ascribed the honour of having discovered the isle of Majorca. At Valldemosa there is a copy of his book, open at the title page. The frontispiece is a drawing of a monastery, pleasant enough to have made me resent the glass case, which prevented me from turning over the pages to look at the other drawings. I later discovered that the book was very scarce and, as it seemed likely that others beside myself might be curious to see what was on the other pages, I decided to reproduce a number of the drawings as illustrations to this book. They do not, I think, have any great distinction, but the "intelligent and laborious" artist, in spite of his friendship with Wagner and other celebrities was scarcely distinguished. Nevertheless the drawings seem to me more satisfactory as decorations, if not illustrations, than photographs, which may be found in any guide book. I have added the two Gustave Doré landscapes for the same reason.

# INDEX